THE FUNCTIONING OF THE FAMILY SYSTEM

ABOUT THE AUTHORS

Gary and Letha Crow live in Xenia, Ohio with their three children. Dr. and Mrs. Crow have been involved in the development and provision of mental health services for children and families for over twenty years and have focused professional research, publication, and training activities in the areas of family functioning and interpersonal adjustment. Readers may also be interested in an earlier publication of the Crows: *Crisis Intervention and Suicide Prevention — Working with Children and Adolescents;* Charles C Thomas, Publisher, 1987.

Dr. and Mrs. Crow are both Licensed Independent Social Workers in Ohio, are Trainers for the Institute for Human Services in Ohio, and have conducted workshops and consultation activities nationally for professionals working with children and families. Mrs. Crow has had faculty affiliations with Ohio Weslyan University in Delaware, Ohio and the Urbana University in Urbana, Ohio. Dr. Crow has been affiliated with the Ohio State University; Wright State University in Dayton, Ohio; The Methodist Theological School in Ohio; and Urbana University in Urbana, Ohio. Dr. Crow is the Executive Director of the Mental Health Resources Corporation in Xenia, Ohio; and The Crow's operate a private training/consultation company: GAC Services.

THE FUNCTIONING OF THE FAMILY SYSTEM

An Educational Approach to Positive Procedures Within Areas of Family Life

By

GARY A. CROW, PH.D., L.I.S.W.

and

LETHA I. CROW, M.S.W., L.I.S.W.

CHARLES C THOMAS • PUBLISHER
Springfield • Illinois • U.S.A.

Published and Distributed Throughout the World by

CHARLES C THOMAS • PUBLISHER
2600 South First Street
Springfield, Illinois 62794-9265

ISBN 0-398-05439-8

Library of Congress Catalog Card Number: 87-32051

With THOMAS BOOKS *careful attention is given to all details of manufacturing and design. It is the Publisher's desire to present books that are satisfactory as to their physical qualities and artistic possibilities and appropriate for their particular use.* THOMAS BOOKS *will be true to those laws of quality that assure a good name and good will.*

Printed in the United States of America
Q-R-3

Library of Congress Cataloging in Publication Data

Crow, Gary A., 1942-
The functioning of the family system : an educational approach to positive procedures within areas of family life / by Gary A. Crow and Letha I. Crow.
p. cm.
Bibliography: p.
Includes index.
ISBN 0-398-05439-8
1. Family psychotherapy. I. Crow, Letha I. II. Title.
RC488.5.C76 1988
616.89'156--dc19 87-32051
CIP

To Sam Kidd and Dan Aultman.

Thank you for your faith in us and
for being people with style, all the time, on purpose.

PREFACE

THE EDUCATIONAL approach to working with families and with the individual members of families may at first seem to be a very novel and innovative approach to family intervention. On the one hand, this perception is accurate. On the other hand, though, experienced counselors, therapists, and others who work with families will quickly recognize an approach that has been an integral part of their practices for a long time. Teaching people how to relate, interact, and participate within relationships has been part of the stock and trade of professionals for many years. This is especially easily seen in work focusing on the parent/child relationship. Generally, emphasis and attention are given to appropriate and inappropriate parenting skills, approaches, and techniques. Similarly, the educational approach has been traditionally used in work with sexual dysfunction or what is in this volume referred to as the "lover dimension" within marriage. The innovative aspect of this book is the extension of the educational approach to the family, family functioning, and individual effectiveness within the family.

The introduction to part one outlines the various sections and activities in the book. We will, thus, not go into detail here about the adventure that lies ahead of you. Instead, we want to take time to first emphasize the positive nature of the educational approach developed here and suggest a few approaches to the book and to the materials included in it.

We have developed what you will quickly find to be a competence-based approach to working within family systems and with family members. The assumption is that many individuals experiencing family-related difficulties simply do not have the insights, skills, and practical understandings needed to function effectively within their families. As noted above, this is frequently seen with parent/child difficulties and with problems related to sexual functioning. We have found through our years of research and clinical experience that a lack of basic skill and competence also applies to other areas of family life. The major goal of the book, then, is to facilitate the involvement of professionals with families in ways that increase interpersonal skill and effectiveness and enhance interpersonal gain and positive feedback within the family system. The goal is to help people become better at being family members, given the complex nature of the family and the multiple relationships operating within the family.

We believe that the book represents a coherent, progressive whole that may be read and appreciated from beginning to end. The nice thing is that it does not need to be approached this way, though. If you choose to read it from the beginning and find yourself getting somewhat bogged down at any point, simply skip on to something that is more interesting or appealing. Alternatively, look at the table of contents, pick out those sections or activities that most catch your interest, and then move directly to them. Each of the four parts of the book and each activity within each of the four parts may easily be considered somewhat independently from the rest of the book. We qualify this by saying "somewhat" since it will be necessary to read all of the materials at some point in time to fully appreciate the full educational approach, although you need not start here.

The activities in Parts Two, Three, and Four are divided into two sections. The first section is the activity itself. The second section is a discussion of the elements in that activity. The discussion sections are primarily intended for professionals who will serve as family system consultants. The first part of each activity is intended for direct use with clients and others with whom you are working. You may use the activity portion as an interview guide, as a discussion guide, as a pencil and paper activity, or as an illustration when making presentations to groups. The idea is that the activity should be used in that way most useful to and meaningful to your client(s).

At first reading, it may seem that the activities are most appropriate for adults. This is generally only true for the activities in part four, with those activities being, in any significant respects, very appropriate for work with adolescents who are contemplating marriage or intimate relationships.

The activities in Part One are primarily intended for use by professionals as guidelines or checklist when working with individuals and families. The activities in Parts Two and Three, though, are very appropriate for both adults and children. In fact, the authors have had excellent success using the activities in Part Two with children as young as four or five years old. The little people are quite capable of learning how to be people with style, all the time, on purpose.

We would like to also take this opportunity to make one additional point. A book is a joint venture an adventure between author and reader. As will be emphasized throughout the text, this principle applies to all relationships and is what we call the principle of reciprocity. In terms of the book itself, the principle of reciprocity says, "We have given the ideas, concepts, and materials twenty years to develop and grow. Added to that is the time spent in preparing what we hope to be a coherent and easy to read book. Our hope is that your reciprocal investment will be to carefully consider the ideas and materials, give them a try, and evaluate the book on the extent to which you have success with its concepts and approaches in your professional practice."

Let us make one additional point. We have had the opportunity to share these materials with hundreds of professionals throughout the United States. A consistent difficulty people experience involves their having difficulty shifting away from a problem-oriented, pathology oriented approach to individuals and families toward the use of positive procedures and competence based techniques. Our educational and training backgrounds press us to diagnose the problem or pathology and then treat that problem or pathology. The educational approach to positive procedures within areas of family life does not follow this type of pathology-oriented diagnosis and treatment approach. Rather, it evaluates and assesses the competence levels of the individuals within the family, with the goal of increasing and enhancing individual competence in ways that result in a net enhancement of general family system functioning and specific interpersonal functioning within the family. If you initially have difficulties with the materials, those difficulties may relate to making the transition from a problem orientation to a positive orientation involving helping people become more skilled and more effective family members.

Thank you for involving yourself in this exciting and reciprocal adventure with us. Use those portions of the materials that fit your style with our good wishes and continuing encouragement. With those portions that do not quite fit your style at this point, consider them and keep in mind that they are available to you. As you develop more experience and success with the educational approach, you will come to find that each of the activities will, in full or in part, find a place in your work with people who are struggling with how to best fit and function within their families.

ACKNOWLEDGMENTS

WE WOULD like to express our appreciation to Steven Winters of the American Health Care Institute for his encouragement and assistance in developing many of the workshops that used these materials as a primary focus for professional consideration. We would also like to express our appreciation to the folks at the Institute for Human Services in Columbus, Ohio for their encouragement and support in our work with professionals primarily dealing with families and children. The opportunity to share the educational approach in full or in part with our professional peers has both enriched and improved the materials, the quality of the materials, and the practical applicability of the materials for professionals as they work with young people and adults.

We would also like to express our appreciation to our associates at the Mental Health Resources Corporation in Xenia, Ohio for their support for and encouragement of our professional activities and the growth and development of many of the concepts and ideas included in this book. Beyond that, our appreciation is extended to the many children and adults we have worked with over the years and for the role they have played in the development of the ideas and concepts included here and in our coming to understand that, for many people, the educational approach to positive procedures within areas of family life is not only a useful approach, it is the best approach.

Finally, we want to extend a heartfelt "thank you" for a job well done to Joanne Phoenix who prepared the final manuscript and to Phyllis Haller who worked on initial drafts and versions of many of the sections and activities in the book.

CONTENTS

PART THREE
THE EDUCATIONAL APPROACH WITHIN PARENT/CHILD RELATIONSHIPS

PART FOUR
BEING MARRIED WITH STYLE, ALL THE TIME, ON PURPOSE

THE FUNCTIONING OF THE FAMILY SYSTEM

PART ONE

THE EDUCATIONAL APPROACH

INTRODUCTION

THE TRADITIONAL APPROACH

AS PROFESSIONAL understanding and intervention skills are focused on families, the dominant approach is based on several assumptions. First the family is seen as an interactive, dynamic system. In this sense, each family member is seen as a participating member of the system and is understood as affecting and being affected by the actions and involvements of all family members. The functioning of the family system, then, is a function of the individual functioning of its members. Second, each member of the family tends to be viewed in relationship to the overall dynamic interaction but also as an autonomous actor in the system. The effect is to understand family problems as functions of both systemic dysfunction and individual psychosocial pathology. The result is a dual perspective conceptualizing family difficulties in terms of system and individual dysfunction. This dualism is frequently resolved by seeing the family as representing the main system, with the individuals in the family representing subsystems.

If the above is pursued one step further, there is a strong tendency to follow a therapeutic approach that treats the individual socioemotional pathology on a diagnosis-treatment basis emphasizing improved psychosocial functioning of the individual and combining this with improved intrasystem (intrafamily) communication. This approach is very effective with disturbed individuals and dysfunctional families. It also requires a lengthy involvement and serious commitment on the part of the family members. Where the involvement and commitment are present, though, the results are frequently remarkable.

For most families and for the majority of people living in family units, the dual approach has several drawbacks. First, the level and degree of commitment and involvement needed from family members are not achievable much of the time. Next, the degree of dysfunction or pathology present in a specific family may not justify the family's seeking or using treatment services. Finally, there may not be anything wrong that should appropriately be understood as representing problems or difficulties needing extended intervention. In any of these cases, treatment as it is traditionally conceptualized is of no benefit to the individual or to his/her family.

AN EDUCATIONAL ALTERNATIVE

The educational approach and materials presented to you are included to meet the needs of families who do not engage with the traditional therapeutic process and procedures. This approach may serve as enrichment activities for many individuals and families and as short-term intervention and consultation activities for those who are having problems but cannot develop adequate commitment and involvement with ongoing individual/family treatment.

Each section of the materials presents a participatory approach to recognizing interpersonal problem points and points of interpersonal strength. The sections also facilitate an educational orientation to positive functioning within areas of family life. The participant sees what works interpersonally, where his/her strengths and weaknesses are, and is assisted in thinking about how to improve his/her functioning. This developed understanding in turn serves as a base for professional consultation and short-term intervention activities.

This approach is suitable with individuals, families, and groups and works well with children, teens, and adults. It also serves well as an identification process for picking out those individuals and families experiencing serious pathology. For the latter, the approach encourages further treatment involvement. Beyond recognition and encouraging further treatment, however, the approach is not appropriate for seriously disturbed individuals and families. It will not hurt. It simply will not help very much.

The materials focus in three family areas; individual functioning of children and adults, parent/child interaction, and marital interaction, understanding that marital is inclusive of whatever adult-adult relationship exists in the particular family. Each section samples those behaviors and other interpersonal elements found in interpersonally effective relationships. The assumption is that the sample will assist the participant and the consultant in identifying interpersonal strengths and weaknesses, with the consultant facilitating understanding of each concept and idea. This assessment and understanding then serves as a base for additional work mutually agreed to by the participant and the consultant.

The recognition and understanding phase is, by itself, useful as a stimulus to more interpersonally effective functioning and relationship enrichment. When followed by short-term consultation and support combined with coaching, the effect for all but the seriously disturbed is almost always significant and frequently remarkable.

When first using the approach and materials, please follow the format for each section carefully being sure to use strategies and techniques appropriate to the age of the participant(s). Also adjust your techniques and strategies to fit the needs of the individual, family, or group with whom you are consulting. As you develop experience with the approach, additions and modifications will naturally develop as a function of your professional style and preferences. It will also be necessary to draw on your knowledge and expertise for specific ideas and suggestions, being sure to maintain the "what works in healthy relationships" approach.

GENERAL STRATEGY

Encourage participants to spend most of their time and energy doing what they do well—maximizing their strengths, minimizing their weaknesses. Help them work on their weaknesses or less strong areas by developing specific techniques and a consistent interpersonal style with which they are comfortable.

Teach people to be proactive and to avoid becoming reactive or simply accommodating to others.

Use the "feel-felt-found" technique. "You seem to feel. . . ." Others have felt. . . . —give examples. We have found that "A-B-C" usually help that type of problem, especially if you stay within your personal style.

Teach participants to maintain their style all of the time with a sense of purpose and commitment.

(Note) The "suggested readings" represent a good source of specific information and ideas that may be used on a "how to" basis with participants.

OVERVIEW

The book is divided into four parts. Part One, which you are currently reading, focuses on the educational approach. Part Two shifts attention to the development of interpersonal style and interpersonal effectiveness at the individual level. Part Three extends interpersonal effectiveness to the parent/child relationship, with Part Four extending interpersonal effectiveness to the marriage relationship. Both Parts Three and Four include additional materials specifically relevant to parents and children effectively relating to each other and spouses relating to each other within what is defined as the internal triangle.

Each part includes a brief introduction followed by a series of activities in which you may engage your clients. The first activities in Part One starts with a series of teaching tips useful when using the educational approach. The next activity in Part One assists in assessing the family system along a continuum from highly functional to highly dysfunctional. The third activity in Part One assist in assessing the readiness of clients to participate in the educational approach.

The first activity in Part Two introduces the idea of style and extends that idea to multidimensional style at the individual level. Clients are then assisted in looking at group roles in which they become involved, developing an understanding of family games that develop even within somewhat more functional families. The third activity assist both youngsters and adults in understanding and thinking about the elements of positive interpersonal style and interpersonal effectiveness. The fourth activity in Part Two then consolidates learning from earlier activities into assisting the client in understanding personal/interpersonal style types and identifying the style type for individual family members.

The activities in Part Two extend next to focus on what is called "the psychology of sharks and seals." This activity begins to separate human nature and socialization, assisting family members in better understanding themselves, each other, and the intrafamily interaction. In the next activity, focus shifts to interpersonal priorities and to increasing priority behavior and feedback for the individual. That activity is followed by focus on interpersonal processes that support and facilitate actualization of the priorities for the individual. Part Two concludes with an activity that assist and encourages the client in self-caring, self-nurturing behavior and involvement.

The first activity in Part Three attends to the rapid assessment of youngsters. Emphasis is given to the point that parenting is not a formula activity. It is, rather, a shared involvement between parents and young people. The next activity in Part Three assist parents in assessing their parenting in relationship to those elements and factors present in effective parent/child relationships. Parents are next assisted in thinking about various approaches to parental authority and considering the optimal authority approach mix from their point of view. That activity is followed by an activity for youngsters to use as they think about and evaluate the parent/child relationship from their point of view. Part Two concludes with an activity entitled "developmental parenting." This activity begins to incorporate the learning from earlier activities and emphasizes the importance of the parent/child relationship's adapting to and accommodating to the development of the child over time.

Part Four brings focus to the marriage relationship. The first two activities in this part focus on partner orientation in relationship to a series of important factors within marriage and marriage balance in terms of a set of traits and characteristics that are important aspects of martial interaction. Those activities are followed by a marriage assessment activity designed to look at both the skill levels and marriage effectiveness of each spouse. Part Four concludes with activities focusing on being friends, being partners, and being lovers within the marriage relationship. The book concludes with an activity designed to teach people about negotiating within relationships and about those skills and techniques useful when negotiating with family members.

PERSPECTIVE DEVELOPMENT

As a final step before moving on to the activities and the focus of the next three parts of this book, you are invited to consider The Us Box.

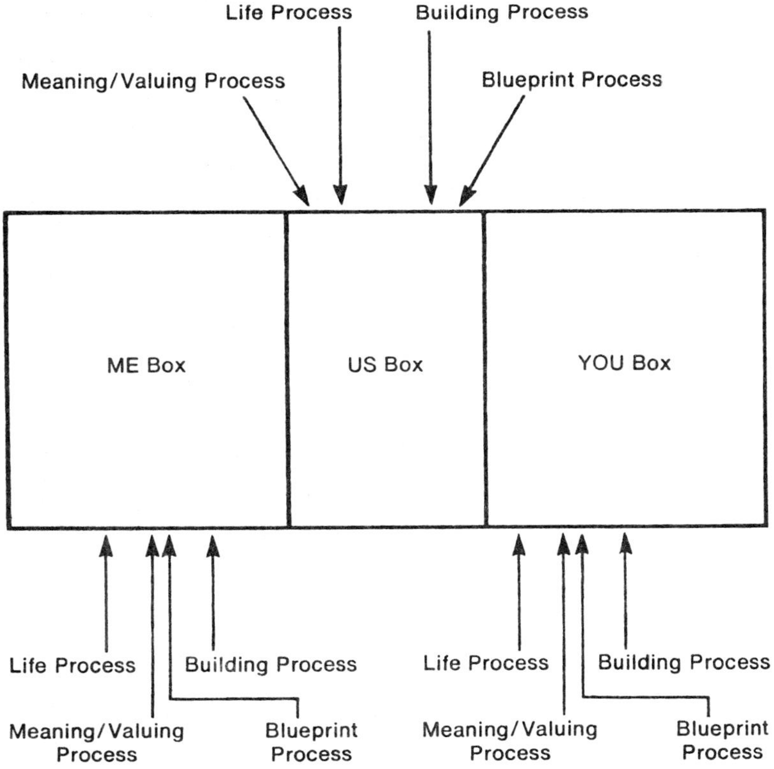

The life, building, meaning/valuing, and blueprint processes merge into the growing and becoming of each individual and into the growing and becoming of their relationship

Severely conflicted relationships are among the most common difficulties confronting everyone in his day-to-day life. Teenagers may find it difficult or impossible to get along with their parents. Husbands and wives may find that they are always fighting, or even worse, they may find that they have nothing to say to each other. Parents may gradually discover or be bowled over by the realization that they can no longer communicate with their children. Friends may drift apart and lose that special feeling for each other, although they may still continue to see each other almost every day. Neighbors may fight, coworkers may not speak to one another, and everyone is uptight. Interpersonal conflict and tension are problems for all of us in varying degrees—maybe only a little bit once in a while or maybe a lot all of the time, perhaps with only one or two people or perhaps with most people. However, often and with however many people, our relationships get messed up. Yours do. Mine do. It is a problem for everyone.

What do we do when our relationship with someone quits working? If that someone is close to us or important to us, we cannot very well just forget about it, ignore him, or pretend there is no problem. Teenagers cannot completely avoid their parents; parents cannot just ignore their children. Husbands and wives cannot simply avoid all contact with each other. Neighbors and coworkers probably cannot cut off all communication. Bad relationships cannot be avoided or ignored in the hope that they will "just go away" by themselves. Willingly or unwillingly, we have to deal with the problem in some way. There are, of course, many styles or patterns of coping with severely conflicted relationships. Some people deal with the problem by yelling. They are experiencing intense and uncomfortable feelings, and they try to force other people into compliance, giving in, changing their behavior, feeling differently, or otherwise acting like they want them to. If you would just straighten up, act your age, not be so unreasonable, behave differently, love me, forget about the past, be more optimistic, not always be nagging, come home earlier, and so on; if you would just change, our relationship would be okay. The yellers attempt to have their way by throwing temper tantrums, threatening, accusing, or otherwise badgering the other individual into changing.

Other people deal with unhappy relationships by falling into the role of the pouter or "stiff upper lipper." Since things are not going the way they want them to go, they withdraw, refuse to communicate, are unhappy, make everyone else miserable, refuse to interact, and are usually "pouting" like small children. They feel that they have been abused, taken advantage of, and that their feelings are not being recognized or responded to. If things do not work out after a while, they stop pouting and take a stiff-upper-lip attitude toward the problem. They will go through the motions but no longer be involved in the relationship. They will fulfill their responsibilities and carry out their duties. They will behave as if everything is fine but will remain emotionally detached from the relationship. In extreme situations, they will play the role of the martyr and feel that they are making a great sacrifice for the sake of the relationship. In other situations, individuals may decide to terminate the relationship through divorce, suicide, running away, firing a good employee, quitting a good job, moving away, and so on. Other people simply attempt to avoid bad relationships by going out of their way to keep from seeing their former friends. Couples continue to live together but "go their separate ways." Parents just "give up" on children and let them have their own way, and so on. The yellers, pouters, stiff-upper-lippers, and quitters are all, in their own ways, trying to deal with severely disturbed relationships.

Perhaps as common as these coping styles are efforts to unwind, unravel, and figure out relationships that are approaching the point of no return. Parents having difficulties with teenage children will attempt to understand how the problem got started when the children were little. They will go over incidents, events, and episodes they feel contributed to the present difficulty. Similarly, couples will look over the years of their marriages trying to find out just where things went wrong. This usually does lead to some level of understanding with the resulting belief that, "if we had it to do over again, we would do things quite differently. Then things would be better now." The people in the relationship focus on "what went wrong" and agree to avoid that specific problem in the future. Things go along fairly well for a while, but then the relationship begins to deteriorate again. Either the same problems occur or new problems come up. Their efforts to repair or "fix" their relationship have not been very successful. Sometimes, of course, this fixing or repairing process is effective. In severely conflicted or extremely deteriorated relationships, however, a small adjustment, a quick repair job, a little fixing is usually unsuccessful. It is a little bit like cooking stew. Sometimes the stew may need a little more salt or a little stir. That works quite nicely when the stew had few problems to begin with. Really bad relationships, though, are like stews made with the wrong ingredients or burned in the process of cooking. A little fixing or a few quick repairs will not help very much.

The reality is that bad relationships, especially when they are close or important relationships, cannot be fixed. They are nonrepairable. This is particularly true of relationships between parents and children, close friends, and husbands and wives.

If relationships cannot be fixed, does this mean that things are hopeless? No, things are far from hopeless. It is actually good news that the relationship cannot be fixed. This allows the possibility of a new relationship where the individuals are more interpersonally skilled, interpersonally effective, and better able to form and maintain relationships that are satisfying and lasting. Fix the old relationship? No, the key is to build a new relationship, a new style of relating to and getting along with each other. Let us look at the nature of relationships and at the reality that unraveling and repairing difficulties within those relationships are insurmountable tasks. With this perspective, we may then move on to completing our consideration of the educational approach and then too learning how to be people with style interpersonally, within parent/child relationships, and within the marriage relationship.

THE NATURE OF RELATIONSHIPS

First, consider two people who do not know each other. What kinds of things must happen to move them from where they do not know each other to where they have a close relationship? The development of a relationship is a complicated and complex process involving many things. As a foundation or first step, individuals must recognize and remember each other. Of the people you have met, how many of their names do you remember? How many would you recognize if you saw them today? Next, how many would recognize and remember you? Thus, people need at least to recognize and remember each other before they can develop a close and important relationship. This point of recognizing and remembering each other can be thought of as point one. From point one, hundreds and thousands of little points must be reached if the relationship is to develop and grow. At each of those points, certain ideas, thoughts, feelings, beliefs, perceptions, notions, attitudes, and assumptions get into the relationship. These may be thought of as small elements or bits that go to make up the relationship. Children learn about their parents' past lives, their personalities, what is acceptable and not acceptable in a relationship, and parents learn an equally wide variety of things about their children. Friends first meet, recognize, and remember each other and then go through a continuing process of adding little bits to their relationship. Relationships come from a growing/developing process that progresses bit by bit.

In relationships between parents and children an important point is relatively easy to see. Just as little bits are continually being added to the relationship, both parents and children are growing and becoming. If we see that along with the process of adding bits to the relationship both people are growing and becoming, we can see that some bits are always being dropped out or omitted from the relationship. As a simple example, when Lee was a baby, his mother had a "bit" in their relationship saying that Lee is unable to walk and needs to be carried. As part of their relationship, then, his mother carried Lee when they needed to go somewhere. As he got older, however, the "Lee-needs-to-be-carried" bit was dropped, and his mother no longer carried him. When Lee was three, he had a bit in his relationship with his mother that said she would help him pick up his toys. He wanted to keep that bit in their relationship, but by the time he was five, his mother had dropped that bit and had put in a bit saying that Lee is old enough to pick up his own toys. When Lee was five, he thought Dad could make anything work out and fix everything. Over time, however, Lee's relationship with his dad changed, and Lee replaced the old bit with a new one that said that Dad has limitations, too. As Mon and Dad watched Lee grow, however, they were also growing and changing. Just as in their relationship with Lee they were always adding and tossing out bits, in their relationship with each other the same kind of process was taking place.

As a matter of fact, it is not difficult to make the generalization that any close and important relationship is always changing and growing. People say, "Things aren't like they used to be between us." You say, "That's normal and healthy. If things were the same as they used to be, that would mean that your relationship has stagnated and is not a viable, living thing." To borrow a term from the palm readers, this growing, developing, maturing, becoming, living process within relationships can be thought of as a relationship's lifeline. It moves, sometimes evenly, sometimes unevenly, but it keeps moving. If it stops, the relationship is, for all purposes, dead. The people may continue living together, they may continue interacting from time to time, they may continue going through the motions. The vital, living relationship is, however, gone.

As we continue our focus on the fact that severely deteriorated relationships are nonrepairable, think about the fact that the two individuals in the relationship are always growing and becoming. They each have a lifeline of their own. The notion of a meaningful relationship is becoming more complex. The relationship has its lifeline, and equally importantly, both individuals have their separate lifelines. Their lives touch each other's; they are concerned with and care about each other; they are involved in an ongoing relationship. Nevertheless, the two individuals are also in pursuit of their own lives.

Both people are continually involved with and care about the lifeline of their relationship. At the same time, their humanness and inherent nature press them toward the pursuit of their lifelines. As this life process continues, the individuals have started at "point one"—they have recognized and remembered each other. From that point on, they continue adding and dropping "bits" into and out of their relationship. Perhaps most of the bits they added and dropped were the same, and were added and dropped at the same time. Inevitably, however, some bits were different, and the timing was not always the same. Both individuals put in and took out some bits different from those put in and taken out by the other person. The result is that the relationship is not made of the same bits for both people. They do not both have exactly the same feelings, ideas, notions, perceptions, attitudes, likes, dislikes, disappointments, and so on, in reference to their relationship. This process of adding and dropping bits may be thought of as the building process.

Just as the relationship has its building process—the adding and dropping of bits over a period of time—each individual has his or her own personal building process. They have specific notions about themselves: attitudes, beliefs, feelings, prejudices, biases; thoughts about how their future will be; expectations for themselves; interests, likes, and dislikes; and so on. As the two individuals grow and become, they have their individual process of deciding who they are, who they want to be, how they ought to be, why they are, and so on. They are separate and distinct individuals. Just as they each have their own life process and their relationship has its life process, they each have their own building process and their relationship has its building process.

The nearly incomprehensible complexity of relationships does not stop here, however. Each bit that is added and dropped within the relationship has its individual meaning and value. A husband may have a bit in his relationship with his wife saying that she is a fair housekeeper. So long as the house does not get into too much of a mess, he may not place very much value on neat and tidy houses. His bit about her housekeeping, then, also has a value that says her being a "fair housekeeper" is fine with him. She may have a bit that says he is too serious and has a poor sense of humor. She may place a very high value on a good sense of humor and thus feels badly about his being too serious.

The examples could be continued to include any bit in the relationship. The point is, though, that every bit in the relationship has both a meaning and a value attached to it. Parents and children may both have a bit in their relationship that says "school is necessary." The parents may place a very high value on school, while the children may see it as less important. This value difference is then a source of conflict in their relationship. They agree that it is important. The disagreement is in terms of "how important." A mother and her teenage daughter may both agree that the daughter's room should be clean. They may have considerable disagreement, however, over the meaning of clean. The mother thinks that "clean" means that everything should be put away and in its place. The daughter feels that "clean" means that the dust should be wiped off enough so that she cannot write her name on the top of her dresser. In any relationship, the meaning and value placed on the bits in that relationship are a potential source of conflict.

In addition to the meaning/valuing process within the relationship, both individuals have their own personal meaning/valuing process. They have their own sense of should and shouldn't, right and wrong, acceptable and unacceptable, appropriate and inappropriate, important and unimportant, and so on. They each have their life process, their building process, and their meaning/valuing process outside of their relationship. These three dimensions are also an integral part of the relationship itself.

A fourth process within the growing and becoming of relationships completes the overwhelming complexity of ongoing, on growing relationships. This fourth process relates to how the individuals put the bits together. Suppose they are sixteen and growing an important relationship between themselves. It is important to each of them that they put the relationship together in a loving and caring way. With sixteen-year-olds, it can be seen that each probably has his or her own notions about how the relationship should be put together. This can be called the "blueprint" process. The blueprint process tells the teenagers how their relationship should be put together, what comes before what, and how the relationship should look at each stage. Both teenagers have some notion about what kinds of things need to happen before others; what kinds of things are and are not acceptable in the relationship; and what different kinds of ideas, feelings, actions, activities, and so on should look like in relation to and in proportion to each other. With husbands and wives, the blueprint process shows how a good relationship would look if they were to achieve one. With friends, the blueprint process has to do with "how we would know a friend if we had one." At a conceptual level, the blueprint process is the organizing, integrating principle within close and important relationships. Of course, along with the blueprint process for his significant and meaningful relationships, each individual has a blueprint for his own life. Each person has a notion about who, what, and where he is; where he is going; why he is going there, and so on. This blueprint process gives meaning and direction to each of his life processes. Similarly, the blueprint process gives meaning and direction to the life process of his relationships.

At the center of a close and important relationship, then, is the life process of that relationship. The building process gives content and substance to the relationship. The meaning/valuing process adds depth and character to the relationship. Finally, the blue print process gives structure and direction. As the relationship grows, each person in the relationship is involved in these same four processes on an individual level, and thus is continually growing and becoming as an individual.

DISCUSSION

As the earlier diagram shows, close and important relationships involve two individuals (me and you) as well as their relationship (us). As the arrows suggest, the life, building, meaning/valuing, and blueprint processes merge into the *US* box, as well as into the *ME* and the *YOU* boxes. The important point here is that when a relationship is "messed up" it is the *US* box that is in severe conflict or not working. Nevertheless, the difficulty may be strictly a result of difficulties in the relationships or it may be a result of difficulties in either the *ME* or the *YOU* box. Alternatively, the relationship problem may arise because the *ME* box has been growing and developing differently and inconsistently with the *YOU* box. In that event, the two individuals are gradually getting to a point where their relationship does not meet their needs, meet their expectations, serve the interest of their growing and becoming, and so on. Compounding the complexity of close and important relationships to the final extreme, consider the fact that even if one truly understood a relationship at a given point in time the processes influencing that relationship are continually changing. This means that the relationship is, itself, continually changing and is never the same. Considering how truly complex the relationship or *US* box really is and that individuals have an *US* box for each of their close and important relationships, the man who says he enjoys an uncomplicated life must be unmarried, work alone, have no parents or children, and have only one friend who just comes around twice a year for lunch. When a relationship is really bad and someone invites you to "try to work things out," it would be the better part of wisdom and understanding to refuse. You might offer instead to build a new relationship, with no effort being made to repair the old one. This is the focus of the following sections of this book: Building new relationships. Emphasis is on relationships within the family; but the skills and techniques to be learned are applicable to a wider variety of relationships and interpersonal situations. The key is to develop and emphasize positive procedures within areas of family life in particular and within one's interpersonal functioning in general. The idea is to become interpersonally proactive and to function interpersonally in ways that maximize the effectiveness, interpersonal gain, and positive social feedback while minimizing counterproductive or ineffective patterns of interpersonal involvement.

ACTIVITY 1

TEACHING TIPS

THIS ACTIVITY is for the trainer to use as a checklist or guide when initiating the educational process with a client or group of clients. Simply answer the questions in terms of the client's involvement with and participation in the learning process. The more responses there are that are less than affirmative or positive, the more problematic the process will be at that point and time. Conversely, clients for whom all of the responses are affirmative or positive are well engaged with the learning process.

The activity should also be used at those points where the learning process seems to be difficult or somewhat problematic. Using the checklist will enable the consultant to pinpoint areas or issues that may be contributing to the difficulty. If so, use the specific question as a guide for clarifying and working out problems within the learning process.

For example, if difficulties develop, the problem may relate to question one. Take time to be sure that the client knows what is expected in both general and specific terms. In addition, be sure that there is a clear understanding of what is expected, with that understanding developed in terms that are meaningful and can be personalized by the client.

1. Does the client know and understand what is expected in both general and specific terms?
2. Does the client know how to do what is expected?
3. Is the new learning related to or extended from things the client already knows, understands, or has previously experienced?
4. Are you emphasizing and reinforcing progress and deemphasizing difficulties or what is left to learn or accomplish?
5. Are you modifying and tailoring your approach and specific goals and content to the unique client?

6. Are you developing and maintaining a positive learning environment for the client?
7. Does the client understand and appreciate why some things are wrong, inappropriate, counterproductive, or ineffective in terms of the client's behavior, actions, attitudes, and so on?
8. Are the steps or learning pieces clear and small enough to make it easy for the client to succeed?
9. Are you accepting as much or more of the responsibility for any progress difficulties as you are attributing to the client?
10. Are you understanding and using what actually motivates the client in terms of that which develops a personal "payoff" for the client?
11. Are you well organized and prepared for each opportunity with the client?
12. Are you remaining consistently calm, patient, and supportive with the client?
13. Do you believe that you understand and are able to work with the client and that he/she understands and is able to work with you?
14. Do you like the client; and do you feel that he/she likes you?
15. Are you managing your relationship with the client in ways that allow that relationship to be used as a standard of comparison from the client's point of view?
16. Are you and the client evaluating and trying to understand why a problem or difficulty has come up in the learning process before trying to do something about it or making suggestions for its resolution?
17. Do you believe that the client can and will make progress?
18. Are you keeping your approach flexible and responsive to the client?
19. Are you consciously using a variety or mix of techniques and approaches?
20. Are you familiar with and do you understand the specific skills and content being taught?

DISCUSSION

This educational approach to positive procedures within areas of family life is centrally a teaching approach. It is, thus, important to first focus on the teaching process itself. The skills, techniques, and other content being taught will be of little value to the client unless he is actively involved in the teaching process and has developed a pattern of interaction with the consultant that facilitates and encourages learning.

The teaching process begins with being sure that the client knows what is expected in specific and general terms. This knowledge must also incorporate a real understanding of what is being taught—what is to be learned. As the client is engaged in the various activities in the educational approach, encourage feedback that lets the consultant know that the client is focused on the activity, knows what the general content area of the activity is, and has a good feel for the elements within the activity in terms of what kind of elements will be involved. For example, a later activity will ask the client to look at his multidimensional style. The consultant should work with the client enough to be sure that the client has a feel for what style is, what the dimensions are within multidimensional, and what kind of statements would be responsive to the activity.

It is also important that the client has some feel for what there is to be learned through the process of completing the activity. For example, the client will learn to look at the six dimensions of his functioning, focus on aspects of those dimensions that are most important to him, and begin to define those aspects in ways that will enable the client to reflect the specific traits and characteristics with style, all the time, on purpose. The result will be a more consistent personal presentation to others, resulting in more consistent, positive feedback from others. Knowing and understanding what is expected within the activity increases the likelihood of the client's serious participation and the likelihood of a positive outcome for the client.

Knowing and understanding what is expected then combines with the client's knowing how to do what is expected. The consultant may want to go through one or two elements of the activity and ask the client to respond verbally. This will enable the consultant to see whether or not the client is responsive, thus implying his knowing how to do what is expected. In a group context, the same teaching goal can be accomplished by having two or three participants respond to an activity item or so verbally before encouraging the group to complete the activity on a pencil and paper basis. If necessary, the consultant can offer two or three appropriate responses, modeling how to do what is expected.

These steps will also avoid the client's getting into the activity and having invested time and energy in the activity only to find out that his participation is inappropriate or nonresponsive. The key to the educational process is the minimization of the possibility of failure or of a nonresponsive investment of time and energy on the part of the client.

The educational approach used here is neither abstract nor disconnected from the day-to-day life and experience of the client. It is, rather, directly related to and extended from things the client already knows, understands, or has experienced. A useful technique in verifying this connection is to simply ask the client, "how does this relate to you and your world today?" A similar technique is to ask, "how does this relate to skills you already have or to strong points in your personality and style of relating to others?" If the client is able to make the connection in fairly concrete terms, all is well. If not, it will be important for the consultant to facilitate the connection process. For example, the client may not immediately make the necessary connection when thinking about his emotional style. The consultant might say, "Tell me something that you feel very strongly about, that you care about, that really makes a difference to you." Once the client has shared the specific content, the consultant can then say, "How do you let other people know about your feelings, know that this really makes a difference to you?" Once the client has shared additional content, the consultant can then say, "The way you share this, the way you express it lets people know what you think but also lets them know how you feel. The "how you feel" is what we call your emotional expression, your emotional style." Once this idea connects with the client, the consultant goes on to say, "Your emotional style is an important part of who you are and has a lot to do with how others relate to you. What can you say positively about your emotional style? To do this, complete the sentence, 'Emotionally I am ________ .' "

As the client and the consultant engage in the process, it is important for the consultant to emphasize the client's progress and to deemphasize any problems or how much there is yet to learn. One way to maximize this strategy is to give almost all emphasis to the learning task in which the client is involved at any time. Comment on the progress the client has made and on your faith in his ability to make similar progress with the content being focused on at this point. The client may say, "I don't think I will ever get on to this. The more I work on it the more it seems like it's going to take forever. I'm not sure I can do it anyway." The consultant might respond, "I can see how you would feel that way. I've worked with a lot of people who have felt the same way at this point. I've found that they usually are not giving themselves enough credit and are forgetting that even a little progress will make a lot of difference in their relationships, in their families. I think you're being too hard on yourself, especially since you have been doing so well."

As the consultant gets more experienced with the educational approach it will become easier and more natural to modify and adjust the approach and techniques to the unique client. Especially at first, however, the consultant may feel a little uneasy about the process. Others who have felt that way have tended to become a little mechanical and distant from the client. It has been found that encouraging the client to take a little more active role in shaping and directing the educational process is a good way to guard against this tendency.

As the client participates within his family and within specific family relationships, one of the goals is to encourage the client to take the role of the other person, look at things from the other's point of view. In the consultation process, this can be done through asking the client, for example, "Now that you see what the idea is, I would appreciate it if we could stop for a couple of minutes so you could help me think about this particular technique or approach. What other ways of going about it can you think of that would be more comfortable to you or that you think most people would relate to more easily?"

In addition, the consultant will find that some clients are more comfortable with a pencil and paper approach while others are more comfortable with a verbal, interactive approach, while still others are more comfortable with the consultant's taking the more active role in the process. For example, a few clients will find it most comfortable if the consultant would go through the entire activity, sharing with the client typical responses to the items, what interpretations might be given to different responses, or how the consultant thinks the client might respond based on the consultant's experience with the client. Some clients are self-starters and ready to take an active role in the process. Others are only prepared to take a quite passive role and must be lead along one small step at a time. Just be sure not to expect the client to be further along the continuum of active and interactive participation than he is at any point in time.

The points discussed above begin to merge into a positive learning environment for the client. Although education is sometimes difficult and frustrating and requires an investment of energy and self, the environment within which the process occurs can and should be a positive experience for the client. Along with positive feedback, affirmation, and an attitude of helpfulness and caring, other aspects of the environment are also important.

Is the client physically comfortable? Is the consultant managing the environment in ways that discourage other people in the situation from pushing, criticizing, or otherwise conveying to the client any sense that the client is not okay and doing okay? Does the environment make it easy for the client to hear and for him to see everyone as they talk or as the client interacts with them?

One technique to be used here is to simply ask the client from time to time if there is anything uncomfortable or negative about the environment, the experience, or about his participation in the process. Importantly, the consultant needs to be quite sensitive here to any subtle or nonverbal clues that suggest that the client may not be being completely open and candid about his feelings and perceptions. A positive learning environment is essential.

Along with knowing what is going well, the client also needs to understand and appreciate why some things are wrong, inappropriate, counterproductive, or ineffective in terms of his behavior, actions, attitudes, and interpersonal participation. When the consultant says to the client, "That particular behavior or action may not be your best choice in this situation," an explanation is in order. First, the message to the client should not be that what he has done or how he has behaved is bad. Rather, the message needs to be that alternative behavior or actions would likely better serve the client's needs, wants, and interest. These ideas and suggestions are, of course, combined with discussion and explanations relative to their value and benefit.

At the same time, the client needs to know and appreciate "why" his current style is not as useful or effective as it might be. A useful technique is to focus with the client in terms of the desired effect or outcome. The approach is always results-oriented. Once the consultant and the client have come to some agreement about the desired results, then it is considerably easier to talk in terms of means to the end, ways of achieving the results. Here, experience is usually the best teacher. Focus on the results the client has been getting. The new or modified approach is an opportunity to possibly achieve results more nearly in line with those desired by the client. At a minimum, the suggested approach may be worth a try, giving the client the opportunity to compare the new results with the results he has been getting. This test is then the participatory explanation as to why the new approach is preferable to the approach that has been used.

Again, the emphasis is in terms of the personal experience of the client and the connection between that experience and the new learning. The consultant wants to consistently avoid any simple appeal to his expertise and experience in ways that suggest that the experience of the consultant is somehow better than or preferable to the life experience of the client.

The consultant's familiarity with the techniques and content may tend to lead to the client's being overwhelmed or feeling as if he should be moving faster than is comfortable. It is, thus, important that the steps or learning pieces are very clear and small enough to make it easy for the client to succeed. Remember that success is always the goal. Among other things this means that the goal should be less understood in terms of general improvement in interpersonal functioning and more understood in terms of the development of specific skills and behaviors. For example, the general goal may be to develop a closer sense of interpersonal involvement between the client and his spouse. Keeping the steps or learning pieces small, the consultant might work specifically on helping the client learn to talk more quietly when interacting with the spouse. Frequently, simply talking more quietly makes it easier for people to develop an increased sense of closeness and intimacy.

As the consultant interacts with the client, it is important that the consultant accept as much or more responsibility for any difficulties or problems related to progress as is attributed to the client. When difficulties arise within any intervention process, there is a strong tendency to attribute the difficulties to the individuals involved. More specifically, the tendency is to see the problem as the client's fault. When using the educational approach, however, "finding fault" is both counterproductive and inappropriate. Rather, the emphasis needs to be considerably less on "why" the problem has come up and considerably more on "what will we do about it."

Extending the point a little, focus is not on "why" things are problematic but on what is accounting for the problematic piece. Once the client and the consultant have the area of difficulty in focus, they then jointly accept responsibility for moving the process along. Sometimes the client takes a little more responsibility; and sometimes, that role is taken by the consultant. The educational approach is a shared process, including shared responsibility. In this sense, the client/consultant relationship models a positive, effective relationship for the client.

As the consultant and the client work together in their shared activity, it is important for the consultant to use that which actually motivates the client in terms of developing a payoff for the client. Here, it is not enough to simply assume that the client is motivated, is interested, and wants to pursue the learning process. A more specific understanding of motivation needs to be developed. Ask the client, "Why do you want to do this? What is in it for you? How do you think you will be better off as a result of the energy and effort you are investing?"

At this important level, attention is on personal payoff or personal gain from the involvement. It is this level of motivation that will sustain the client at those points when the process may become difficult, when learning is somewhat less than easy, and when it comes time to practice and practice again. At these points, the consultant, knowing what the payoff is, can bring the client's attention back to the payoff, can use the payoff as delayed reinforcement, and can point out to the client those points at which the client actually gets the payoff, receives the personal benefits of the process. These points may be small and can easily go unnoticed by the client, since recognizing positive feedback from others and responding to it may be part of the difficulties themselves. For example, if the client perceives having his child be more cooperative as something that would increase the general comfort level of the client, progress may be hard to see at those points when the level of cooperation is quite low. Knowing that the level of cooperation develops personal payoff for the client, it may be possible to point out to the client that the points of low cooperation are getting fewer and farther between. The consultant might be able to say, "I can tell that you are feeling really quite frustrated right now. It feels like there is no cooperation at all. At times like this, it is hard to remember that you really are making progress. I did note as you were talking, though, that you and your son had been working together for almost two hours before the bottom dropped out of the cooperation level. Progressing from five minutes without things falling apart to two hours is an amazing amount of progress in such a short period of time. You should be really pleased with how well you are doing, even though it does feel frustrating right now."

As the consultant moves through the educational process, it is important for him to be well organized and prepared for each opportunity with the client. This preparation takes several forms. First, it is important to have in mind specific learning activities and opportunities that fit with the needs and interests of the client. Of course, this teaching plan will be modified and influenced by the particular interest and focus of the client during any educational episode. Nonetheless, preparation includes an individualized lesson plan including the most likely points to be covered, techniques to be developed, and other specific content.

In addition, the consultant needs to look at the educational opportunity relative to both the client and the other members of the client's family. At times, "what would be most useful to other family members" strongly influences the approach on any given occasion. Beyond that, the lesson plan should take into consideration past involvement of the client, where the client is likely to be personally and interpersonally at the beginning of the session, and which small pieces and little bits are likely productive points to pursue. The educational approach is not a happening or existential encounter. It is, rather, a planned and guided learning experience.

As part of the consultant's style, consistent calmness, patience, and supportiveness with the client are important. The key here relates to the more general importance of a positive learning environment. The point may seem small but is actually central to the process. The client's emotional state will tend to fluctuate or vacillate. It is, thus, important that the consultant remain reasonably calm and even dispositioned avoiding any tendencies to become anxious, hostile, aggressive, frustrated, disengaged from the process, or to convey any other feelings or emotions that might tend to alienate the client or cause him to begin to react negatively to the consultant. The consultant's feedback to the client is always neutral to positive.

The point extends to patience on the part of the consultant. The client learns that his idiosyncratic pace will allow him to understand and respond to some things more quickly than others and will not always reflect smooth and continuous progress. Patience on the part of the consultant conveys an acceptance of the client, the client's progress or lack of it at any point in time, and conveys a sense of respect and appreciation for the client. Calmness and patience combine with positive interaction and feedback to support who the client is, how the client is doing, and the effort the client is making. The supportiveness of the consultant is, perhaps, as important as any other single attribute of the client/consultant relationship. The role model being projected for the client is of similar value.

Believing that he understands and can work with the client and that the client understands and can work with the consultant are additional essential ingredients in the educational approach. The dynamic here tends to operate as a self-fulfilling prophecy. To the extent that there are mutual understanding and mutual faith between the client and the consultant, the process will tend to succeed. To the extent that either perceives a lack of understanding or experiences a lack of faith in the other, the process will suffer. It is also clear that the self-confidence and self-esteem of the consultant are important aspects of a positive learning environment. The usually unspoken message to the client is, "Through what I say and do, I am conveying to you my understanding of you, your needs, and your interest. This understanding combines with the belief on my part that I can help you learn." This confidence is picked up by the client and is through identification, translated into the client's belief in himself. The interaction of mutuality and shared belief, then represent powerful positive drivers that move the process along.

At a more personal level, mutuality and shared belief translate into a sense that the client and the consultant like each other. When engaged with families, this becomes an even more complex part of the process since the development of a "we like each other" pattern of interaction needs to be developed with each family member. Of course, the shared feeling will be stronger between some family members and the consultant than with others. Nonetheless, serious difficulties can quickly develop at any point that the "we like each other" understanding does not develop or begins to breakdown. This is a point that is usually best approached directly. The consultant might say, "I get the feeling that you don't like me very much right now." Always add the "right now" in order to draw attention to the immediate point of interaction. Alternatively, the consultant may on some occasions need to say, "Right now, I am feeling that I do not like you very much. I really want for us to spend some time talking about that so that we can get past this point with each other." The discussion then needs to focus in terms of specific behaviors or self-projections that seem to be contributing to the perceptions. The point in the process is, in short, managed as an important learning opportunity for both the consultant and the client.

The underlying theme here is for the consultant to manage his relationship with the client in ways that allow the relationship to be used as a standard of comparison from the client's point of view. It is also important for the consultant to facilitate and encourage the comparison. For example, if the client and the consultant should reach a "we do not like each other" point, focus on that point and successfully work it through in terms of a more positive interaction. This process then becomes a referent or "how to" example for the client.

If the client is experiencing negative gain in one of his family relationships, the consultant might say, "This is a little like when you and I were talking about liking and not liking each other. I was impressed with the skill with which you were able to work through that point in our relationship. It seems to me that the same skills could be used by you in this situation in your family. What do you think?" Sensitivity to potential points of comparison will increase the opportunity for the consultant to reinforce this use of the consultant/client relationship. Progress is evident when the client begins to make the comparisons spontaneously.

Given the best effort on the part of both the client and the consultant, difficulties and problem points will arise. The important point here is for the consultant and the client to evaluate and try to understand why a problem or difficulty has come up in the learning process before trying to do something about it or making suggestions for its resolution. It is tempting to assume no one would try to resolve a problem before understanding what the problem is and what may account for it. Nonetheless, this type of response, trying to fix before understanding what needs fixed, occurs more frequently than one might think.

Falling into the trap, the consultant hears the client say, "I am having a problem with this." The immediate response on the part of the consultant is, "You ought to try. . . ." Alternatively, the client says, "I am having a problem with this. I think I will. . . ." The issue is that the solution is simply a response to having a problem but is not clearly related to an understanding of or sensitivity to the problem. The client should be discouraged from this approach either within the consultation relationship or within his family involvements.

Taking time to evaluate and understand the problem point avoids the real likelihood that the client will simply use old strategies, old approaches, and habitual ways of responding. Better are responses that are thought out, related to an understanding of the problem, and developed as a specific way of handling or working through a specific set of problems, difficulties, or interactional tension points. If a problem is worth responding to at all, it is worth the extra thought and attention it will take to respond in ways that maximize the likelihood of effectively and positively resolving the problem along with minimizing the likelihood of the difficulty's recurring.

A point already made in other ways needs reiterated in more specific terms. It is important that the consultant believes that the client can and will make progress. One way of approaching this is to go beyond the level of intuition and subconscious perception to develop a chart listing the strengths and assets the client already has that will be useful and beneficial in terms of progressing through the learning process. This listing approach is best accomplished in conjunction with specific later activities and includes those areas of strength, special ability, or interpersonal capacity emphasized in the activity. A similar listing should be developed in terms of those factors, characteristics, or other elements that result in the consultant's belief that the client will make progress. The two list combine to develop an analysis of what might be thought of as the client's progress potential. The same approach can then be used in making two lists including elements related to what might be thought of as the client's failure potential. The task of the consultant is then to actualize the client's progress potential and to minimize the interference or deterrent capacity of the client's failure potential. More specifically, this type of approach assist the consultant in maximizing strengths and minimizing weaknesses. The educational experience should then be directed to the elements of the client's progress potential and away from his failure potential.

In order to accomplish the above, the consultant must keep the approach flexible and responsive to the client. He must be especially alert to any appearance of elements related to the client's failure potential and prepared to deal with those comments in ways that minimize their effect or impact. At the same time, the consultant needs to be able to shift to focus on progress potential elements. Making the same point in somewhat different terms, if elements within the client's failure potential begin to appear and or interfere with the process, it is clear that the process is emphasizing counterproductive elements, resulting in less than useful responses and reactions, or focusing in areas with which the client is not yet ready to deal. An important part of flexibility, then, is the ability to back away from the current approach and content and toward more productive and useful areas.

There will be times when it is important to change methodologies, activities, or other aspects of the approach to develop more concert or a better fit with where the client is at the specific point in time. For example, if the client seems to be getting bogged down, appears to be resisting the process, and doesn't seem fully responsive to what is happening at the time, it may be useful to shift focus to some of the earlier points in this discussion, move from one activity to another, go back to activities that had been processed earlier, change methodologies from more verbally oriented approaches to paper and pencil oriented approaches, or simply suspend the process long enough to talk with the client for a few minutes about how he is feeling and what the process looks like from his point of view at the time.

The above is facilitated through consciously using a variety or mix of techniques and approaches. This helps for two reasons. First, the variety will be more interesting and stimulating to the client. Second, using a variety or mix gives the consultant the opportunity to both tailor the approach to the client and develop experience with those techniques and approaches to which the client responds most effectively and positively. Beyond that, the strategy presents to both the client and the consultant the opportunity to deal with the same concepts, techniques, and content areas using different methodologies. This facilitates learning through repetition as well as learning through developing and understanding that several approaches can and do lead to nearly equivalent ends. The effect is to expand and extend the learning experience for the client in ways that most nearly assure that the client will be able to identify with the learning process, the content, and the approach. The modeling value of this strategy for the client is also important, especially in terms of his learning to use a variety of techniques and approaches within family relationships.

The key to all of the above is the consultant's understanding of and familiarity with the skills and content being taught. Teachers must be able to teach but they must also be very familiar with that which is being taught. Most consultants will be very familiar with most of the content areas and with most of the skills and techniques being taught. It will also be important for them to supplement this knowledge and understanding through reading and continuing training. In addition, it will also be useful and at times critical for the consultant to assure the availability of other consultants with whom the client is able to interact relative to specific content or skill areas.

For example, functioning as a lover within the marriage relationship requires specific knowledge and skills related to the sexual functioning of men, of women, and of sexual interaction between men and women. The same is true in terms of parent/child relationships, especially where the child involved has some type of special problem or difficulty. The consultant need not be all things to all people. It is enough to have a good knowledge and skill foundation and a willingness to seek out and make available other resources that may be needed by the client.

ACTIVITY 2

ASSESSING FAMILY SYSTEM FUNCTIONING

THIS ACTIVITY is designed for use by the consultant in assessing the level of dysfunction or disorganization within the family. It has been adapted from a more general organizational crisis model and has real utility for determining whether or not the family can benefit from this educational approach. The activity identifies six variables on which the family is to be evaluated by the trainer. Below each variable are four descriptors related to the variable. Through observation and discussions with the family, the trainer should simply determine which descriptor best describes the family in terms of the variable in question. For example, are family relationships best described as fragmented, protective, supportive, or interdependent. For trainers for whom the descriptors do not quickly communicate the concept or idea, reading the discussion that follows the activity may be useful as a preliminary to completing the activity for a specific family.

Once the family has been rated on all six variables, simply add together the numerical values of the descriptors checked. This will result in a family assessment score from six to twenty-four. Generally speaking, families who function in the upper third of the range (19-24) are excellent candidates for this educational approach. Families who function in the lower third of the range (6-12) may derive some benefit from the approach but will need interventions that are considerably more comprehensive and therapeutically powerful. The trainer will probably get somewhat mixed results with families in the middle third of the range.

Simply check the appropriate descriptor, noting that the number of the descriptor represents the numerical value for that descriptor.

Relationships
1. Fragmented
2. Protective
3. Supportive
4. Interdependent

Communication
1. Random
2. Ritualized
3. Serial (searching)
4. Congruent

Problem Solving
1. None
2. Mechanistic
3. Explorative
4. Flexible

Extrafamilial Relationships
1. Disconnected
2. Alienated
3. Reciprocal (mutuality)
4. Coordinated

Decision Making
1. Paralyzed
2. Autocratic
3. Participatory
4. Task centered

Planning
1. None
2. Expedient
3. Synthesizing
4. Integrative

DISCUSSION

Focus here is on the six variables and twenty-four descriptors included in the above activity. The first variable focuses on the *relationships* within the family, on how family members relate to each other. This can be understood at two levels. First, understanding can be developed in terms of the pattern of interaction; and second, understanding can be developed in terms of the function or value of the interaction to the individuals and to the family system. Each of the four descriptors relates to both levels.

Fragmented relationships show very little pattern and reflect little continuity or consistency over time. They are, thus, not continuously available to family members and serve little useful function within the family system. In fact, fragmented relationships are incompatible with a systemically functioning family insofar as the relationships or connections between people need to be relatively continuous in order for the interaction of the individuals to develop as a functioning system.

Fragmented relationships represent the most dysfunctional level of family functioning. A somewhat improved level of functioning is seen in families where relationships are characterized by a protective pattern and function. At this level, the pattern is such that family members are fairly continuously available to each other, with that availability primarily characterized by an orientation to protecting family members both from other family members and from external influences and factors. This is basically a defensive orientation and may be characterized by a clinging quality where family members relate to each other as a way of protecting both themselves and each other from perceived threats or factors that are generally understood as out of their control. When thinking about the family as a system, this level of functioning at least serves to protect and maintain the components—family members—of the system and serves to further the continuation of the system. As can be seen, the relationships at this level do, at least, serve a useful function for the family and its members.

At the next higher level of functioning, the protective aspect of relationships continues but those relationships also serve a supportive function for the family members. At this level, relationships facilitate positive interpersonal gain and the family relationships serve both the interest of the system and the interest of the family members in terms of their activities, involvements, and participation within and outside of the family. Families functioning at this level might say, "We help and encourage each other."

At the highest level of functioning, family relationships are best described as interdependent. At this level, the pattern reflects a truly systemic interactive pattern within the family. The functions of protection and support are still present; except family relationships have extended to incorporate the full range of needs and interest of each family member. Family members can comfortably and confidently count on each other and also understand that the welfare and well being of each family member is significantly dependent on the welfare and well being of the family and the other family members. At this level, relationships might also be described as complimentary and additive. The strengths and abilities of each family member are understood as resources available to all family members, with the less strong areas for each family member finding compensatory support in the abilities and capacities of other participants in the system.

At the optimal state, the "self" of each family member is a function of her autonomy combined with her membership in and participation in the family. At this level, families might say, "We are all very unique individuals but are also part of our family. Both parts of who we are must be understood and recognized if you are to know us well."

A similar hierarchy of functioning levels applies to *extrafamilial* relationships. At the most dysfunctional level, these relationships are best characterized as disconnected. The parallel to fragmented intrafamilial relationships is obvious. In extrafamilial terms, relationships are simply not such that there are good connections with external resources, institutions, support systems, or other individuals or entities that might serve the interest of the family and its members if they were more readily available. Here, relating to a consultant is problematic insofar as the family and its members have difficulty developing a relational connection with the consultant.

At the next higher level of functioning, extrafamilial relationships may be characterized as alienated. Here, the relationships exist but do not serve the needs and interest of the family and its members. The perception is one of alienation or nonbelonging—nonparticipation. The family and its members are fairly constantly turned off or rebuffed by external individuals and entities or at least perceive themselves in these terms. Families who operate at this level tend to take a somewhat fatalistic approach to dealing with anyone outside of the family, having very low expectations for those relationships and connections.

At the next higher level of functioning, extrafamilial relationships may be understood as reciprocal or characterized by mutuality. It is a quid pro quo orientation to the external world. For example, a reciprocal orientation might operate in a specific situation in this way. A youngster is having difficulties in school or is in need of special services. The parents' orientation to the school is from the perspective that the school "has to" provide the services or respond to the needs because the parent pays taxes and the laws say that the school must do what is needed. The same client working with a consultant may think that the consultant is being nice and trying to be helpful simply because she is getting paid to do so. One helps one's neighbor because neighbors help each other as a reciprocal requirement for being neighborly. The same orientation then holds for other interactive experiences between the family and family members on the one hand and external entities and individuals on the other hand.

At the highest level of functioning, extrafamilial relationships may be best seen as coordinated. The idea is to coordinate external resources, opportunities, and interests in ways that respond to the needs and interest of the family and its members. Here, the consultant is nice and is helpful because that is who and what the consultant is. That resource then matches up with the needs and interest of the family. Arrangements are then made that enable the consultant to consult and the family to receive the consultation services.

At school, the child is helped because that is or at least ought to be the nature of the professional resource. If some resource exchange is required in order to facilitate the coordination, the exchange will be made, e.g., the payment of consulting fees. At this level of functioning, the family's paying the consultant is only incidental to the process.

Communication is the next focal variable. At the most dysfunctional level, communication among family members is random. Again, note the parallel with fragmented relationships. Random communication is, of course, ineffective and inconsistent in relationship to the family as a system. To the extent that the primary linkage or connection between family members is in terms of communication, random communication represents an absence of any identifiable pattern, of any significant systemic interaction within the family. People may talk and interact in both verbal and nonverbal ways. Nonetheless, these episodes of communication serve no dependable, continuing, or particularly useful function, although it may help the people avoid becoming bored and totally alienated from each other.

At the next higher level of functioning, communication is ritualized. Here it will help to draw the analogy to other types of rituals, such as social rituals. People are communicating out of habit, as a function of the accepted patterns or procedure, or by following the unwritten family rules. For example, in families where ritualized communication is the norm, one quickly gets the feeling that everyone has heard and participated in the conversation before. In addition, each family member is well schooled in terms of her role and expected participation in the communication of the family.

At the next higher level of functioning, family communication is best described as serial or searching. Conversations tend to drift and usually do not maintain any clear focus for long. If the topic is important or of interest to the participants, one gets the impression that family members are searching for ideas, feedback from others, or new ways of thinking or perceiving. Ordinarily, though, the process does not go beyond this searching-exploratory activity.

At the most functional level, communication is best described as congruent. Here, there may be some ritualized communication, an initial pattern of searching or exploratory communication, but the end result of the process will be the development of congruence. People are talking about the same thing at the same time in approximately the same terms. At this level, one also notes a real capacity to focus on particular problems or issues, the needs and interest of specific family members, or other topics of interest to the participants. It is as if the communication process leads to a collective consciousness, a collective capacity to think about and deal with the problem, opportunity, situation, or other specific topic.

Decision making enters the family system as the next variable. At the most dysfunctional level, decision making within the family system may be described as paralyzed. Problems and issues come up from minor to major, with those in authority simply being unable or unwilling to make necessary decisions. Frequently, decisions are made simply by default or as a function of not deciding; or actions taken are based on impulse, minimal thought, and are generally unrelated to the family's overall welfare or well being.

At the next higher level of functioning, decision making is simply autocratic. In this sense, decisions are frequently arbitrary and seldom take into consideration the feelings and interest of the family and of its members.

At the next higher functional level, decision making is participatory, with family members having a voice in the process. At this level, the participants in the process generally make the final decisions, although the autocratic approach is still sometimes used. At the highest level of system functioning, decision making is task-centered. At this level, the decision maker and the process depend on the specific task or purpose for the decision. Generally, the individual having the direct responsibility for the effects of the decision will make the decision. Much of the time, decisions are simply made by the person who needs the decision at the time. Of course, the participatory process and occasionally the autocratic process also operate; but the preponderance of decision making rest with those most directly involved and effected. As a variation on the task-centered theme, the decision making process may also be categorized, with specific family members making decisions within given categories, e.g., household decisions, minor financial decisions, major financial decisions, business-related decisions, and within other categories important to the specific family.

Central to the life of the family system is *problem solving,* with this important aspect of family life being best described as "none" within the most dysfunctional family systems. Problems are simply not solved in any active and intentional way and especially not in any way that takes into consideration the needs and interest of the family and its members. At this level, problems tend to accumulate and intensify purely as a result of nonattention to them.

At a somewhat more functional level, problem solving within the family is best described as mechanistic. The process is somewhat mechanical and incapable of innovation, novel solutions, and highly individualized solutions to new or unfamiliar problems. Also, the same solution tends to be given for the same problem even if the special conditions or circumstances at the time should reasonably be expected to call for an individualized solution. At the next higher level of system functioning, problem solving becomes explorative. Here, note the parallel to the "searching" level of communication within the family systems. At this level, the family continues exploring for solutions to problems and for resolutions of difficult situations. The exploration continues until a solution is developed that seems to fit or respond to the problem. The result is not necessarily what would have been the best solution but represents a very adequate solution on a one-problem-at-a-time basis.

At the highest level of problem solving, the appropriate descriptor is flexible. Here, all of the processes discussed may be used with the addition of the capacity to flexibly use different approaches to different problems. It is a little like having a problem-solving tool kit. The flexible approach says that if pliars do not seem to fit the problem, a screwdriver may be tried. Also, this level of functioning allows for the use of new tools that are not already in the problem-solving tool kit.

Perhaps *planning* is the variable that most typifies the family style and the level of functioning of the family system. At the most dysfunctional level, there is no planning and things just tend to happen. The family and its members begin to take on a somewhat chaotic pattern of interaction and a somewhat fatalistic philosophy of life. At a somewhat improved level of functioning, planning becomes expedient. At least here thought is given to what will work or get the family where they are going in the short run. The planning takes in few issues beyond the immediate need or interest; but at least that need or interest is usually responded to at some level.

At the next higher level of functioning, planning may be described as synthesizing. The needs and interest of the family and its members are added into the process as they develop and are responded to in terms of the available resources, given those things to which resources are already committed. Here, resources include money but also include time, energy, and available motivation. At the highest level of functioning, planning is best described as integrative. Here, the needs and interest of the family and its members are identified, prioritized, and considered in relationship to all aspects of family life. New pieces are not simply added to the existing list. They are carefully considered in relationship to all current aspects of family life, the history of the family with similar needs and interest, and—here is the key—in relationship to all anticipated needs and interests of the family that may develop in the future. Any new piece that enters the family system is then part of the system as a whole and not something that has been appended to an already existing and in place system. Of course, not all can be anticipated; and part of the integrative planning process is to allow enough flexibility to always be able to respond to the unexpected, within limits.

(Note) The above discussion focuses on the family as a whole, the family as an entity. As has been noted, families functioning within the most dysfunctional range are, in fact, not operating as viable, positive systems. They are, rather, operating as a collection of loosely related individuals. In contrast, families functioning at the higher levels represent true systems in the interdependent, interactive sense of the term.

As you assess families, though, there is an additional factor to keep in mind. Even though the family itself may be quite dysfunctional, there may be family members or specific relationships within the family that are significantly more functional than the family as a whole. For example, a family with a chemically-dependent member may be quite dysfunctional when looked at as a single entity. When other family members are considered individually, though, it may be that their functioning levels are atypical in reference to the family as a whole. Similarly, some of the specific relationships within the family may be quite positive and viable. For these basically dysfunctional families, the educational approach may be most appropriately used on an individual basis with more functional members or in terms of specific focus on the more functional relationships. Understanding the family as a system leads to the positive factor that, enhancing or improving the function of any element within the system has a net positive effect for that system. Helping specific family members and working on specific family relationships will have a net positive effect even for highly dysfunctional family systems.

ACTIVITY 3

ASSESSING CLIENT READINESS

RATE THE client in terms of the thirteen statements below. Use a scale from five to one with five equals very high, four equals high, three equals medium, two equals low, and one equals very low. Once all thirteen ratings have been made, add the ratings together and divide by thirteen. The result will be a readiness score from one to five. Clients rating 4.0 or higher are very ready for participation in the educational approach to areas of family life. Clients rating 2.0 or less are not ready and will benefit from a more supportive, less directive approach designed to increase readiness along the thirteen variables. The trainer will likely experience mixed results relative to readiness with clients whose readiness scores fall in the middle portion of the range.

In addition to the readiness assessment, this activity may be used with the client to discuss the educational approach, its strengths and limitations, and the client's potential participation in the process. Also, the activity is quite useful when difficulties develop in the process. Frequently, those difficulties relate to issues and areas raised in this activity.

1. The client expects the process to succeed.
2. The client has a realistic vision of or perception of success—how things will be when the process succeeds.
3. The client is motivated by the likely payoff or outcome of the process.
4. The client places high personal value on obtaining the payoff or likely outcome.
5. The client understands that—in the long run—it will take as much time and energy to maintain the status quo or current situation as it will to succeed through the educational process.
6. The client takes responsibility for his participation and interaction within the family system.

7. The client understands his active role and influence within the family system.
8. The client believes in his ability to make the commitment and changes necessary for success.
9. The client has generally positive self-esteem.
10. The client generally likes other family members.
11. The client is looking beyond simple self-interest in the process' succeeding.
12. The client sees each family member benefitting from his participation in the process.
13. The client is realistic about his abilities, skills, and capacity to function within the family in an effective way.

(Note) This activity may be simply used as a checklist for the trainer. In addition, it may be used as an interview questionaire or as a group activity when working with groups. In this case, the trainer should rephrase the items to fit the setting. For example, item 1 could be changed to read, "I expect the process to succeed." The client could then respond verbally in terms of his expectations. Within a group context, group participants could simply number from 1 to 13 and put their rating beside the appropriate number. For example, if the group participant strongly expected the process to succeed for him, a "5" would be put beside the number one. With this modification, the remainder of the instructions relative to the activity remain the same.

DISCUSSION

It will be helpful to consider the discussion following activity 1 in conjunction with the discussion here. The teaching process as developed in activity 1 parallels very closely this activity and the readiness of the client to participate in the educational process.

The client's expecting the process to succeed is essential to whether or not the process will, in fact, succeed. The more optimistic the client is, the more energy and effort he will attempt to invest and the more receptive he will tend to be to the concepts, suggestions, and techniques to be learned. Conversely, the client's believing that the process will not succeed makes it very difficult for both the client and the consultant. It may be that the client will participate in the process enough to begin to develop some success and make some progress which may in turn alter his thoughts and feelings about the educational approach. Even while making this initial investment, though, the consultant needs to explore with the client his initial pessimism. Frequently, it will relate to previous experience with intervention efforts, misperceptions the client may have about the consultant or the educational approach, or a sense of futility in relation to having any ability to change or modify relationships or responses of other people in the family.

Even if the client expects the process to succeed, it is important for the consultant to clarify success. It may be that the client expects to succeed but that his perception or idea about success is unrealistic or in some other way inconsistent with what success will be like. In the role of the consultant, you might say, "I am pleased that you feel that things will get better and that your interpersonal skills will improve. Talk with me a little about how you see things when the process succeeds." Through this step, the consultant and the client can clarify the likely outcome of the process to better assure that the client will feel positive and successful as a result of the process. It is also important to enter into the educational approach without minimizing the possibility that either the client or the consultant could perceive the process as succeeding without the concurrence of the other.

This point extends to the motivation of the client. Once it is understood what success will be like, the consultant and the client can then evaluate the extent to which the client is motivated by the likely outcome or "payoff" of the educational involvement. At the optimal level, the client's motivation will focus in three areas. First, he will be motivated by increasing interpersonal skill and effectiveness. This achievement will be personally satisfying. Second, motivation will come in terms of improved interpersonal relationships and more comfortable interpersonal involvement with other family members. Third, motivation will come in terms of the increased comfort and satisfaction of other family members. Based on a realistic understanding of the likely outcome, all three payoffs blend into the major interpersonal gain and motivational energy for the client. If any of the three motivational areas are seen as unnecessary or as unimportant by the client, the success of the educational approach is proportionally less assured.

As can be seen from the above, focus here is on the client's placing high personal value on the outcome or payoff. The client says, "All three areas are very important to me." The personal valuing of the outcome, the enhancement of family relationships, and the increased satisfaction and comfort of other family members are then the payoff for the investment of time and energy.

The educational approach is time consuming for the client and requires a lot of energy and self-directed effort. Here, though, an additional reality needs to be introduced and discussed between the consultant and the client. In the long run, it will require as much time and energy to maintain the problematic status quo—to keep things the way they are—as it will to use the educational approach to improve things for the client, other family members, and the interpersonal involvements of family members. Problematic and negative interactions within the family are energy draining and time consuming, with the investment of time and energy achieving little. The educational approach is then a substitute way of using the family resources that, in the long run, will reduce the negative drain or ineffective use of family time, energy, and other resources. It is, then, an investment in the future for each member of the family.

In assessing client readiness, attention now shifts away from understanding success and the payoff for the client to developing and understanding of the client's participation in the family. Does the client take personal responsibility for his participation and involvement within the family system? The point being pursued here with the client is subtle and may seem minor but is actually essential to the educational approach. The client is going to learn to be a proactive component within the family system, an individual who interacts with style, skill, and purposefulness. Specifically, this orientation will develop in terms of his individual functioning and specifically in relationship to his children and spouse. In order to do this the client needs to understand and accept responsibility for his involvement and participation.

There is no intent to change other members of the family or to see one's self as simply reacting to other family members. Instead, the client is understood as an active ingredient within the system, as a responsible and self-directed family member.

Many clients will understand their active role and influence within the family and will accept personal responsibility for both. Other clients, however, will need specific consultation attention directed to defining and clarifying their intrafamily role. Usually, role clarification is somewhat less at issue than understanding and clarifying the multiple influences that the client has within the family. Most of the time, it is enough to aquaint the client with the concepts and with a few of their implications within the family system. This familiarization leads rather quickly to the client's generalizing the concepts and ideas throughout his participation in the family. Some attention to this point has the secondary benefit of better aquainting the client with the inductive nature of the educational approach. Understanding more specific and concrete areas of functioning and then generalizing that understanding to broader family areas and issues.

As an outcome of the educational approach, the client will begin to modify his behavior, involvement and participation within the family. Gradually, the small modifications will lead to more general changes in the client's style, approach, and functioning. It is important that the client believes in his ability to make the needed commitment and changes. Important to this step is the consultant's belief in the client and faith in the client's ability. The positive element here is that virtually anyone who is willing to make the initial commitment will quickly learn that he does have the necessary ability.

The key here actually has more to do with the client's level of self-esteem than with actual ability. When the consultant is working with an individual who questions his — the client's — ability, it is important for the consultant to understand that the issue is more in terms of the client's self-esteem. If this area is problematic, the consultant will want to spend some time in a supportive way reenforcing the client's interest, desire to have better relationships, and demonstrated interest in his family. The consultant might say, "I hear what you're saying and understand that you do not feel real confident in your ability. I have worked with other people who have felt the way you do. I've found that people who care as much about their family as you seem to care are usually successful with the educational approach if they will invest a little initial time and energy. What do you think? I think you will be able to make progress because you really want things to be better. Shall we give it a try and see how it goes?"

An additional factor enters in here that also needs to be worked through. The prognosis for success is much higher for clients who generally like the other members of their families than for those who do not. Recall the three areas of payoff: improved personal functioning, improved relationships, and increased comfortableness and satisfaction for other family members. If the client is involved in the educational approach in part for other family members, liking or disliking other people in the family makes a difference. He is more likely to be motivated to help people who are liked than those who are disliked.

Disliking a specific family member presents a learning opportunity in terms of understanding the behavior, attitudes, or pattern of involvement of the other person that evoke dislike or negative reactions. If the consultant can facilitate understanding at this level, progress is already being made.

For example, suppose an ingredient of why the client dislikes another member of the family has to do with the other member's habitually saying negative, demeaning, and hostile things to the client. First, simply beginning to isolate the specific behaviors and attitudes is itself consistent with the educational process. The client sees what the other person is doing that evokes the negative reaction. Next, the consultant begins to work with the client in terms of alternative behaviors and responses that enable the client to feel more in control and to experience less perceived assault to his self-esteem. For example, maximizing the use of the elements of positive interpersonal style discussed later may be useful. Keep in mind, though, that the goal here is not to change the behavior of the other person. It is rather to facilitate the client's developing better defined style and increased interpersonal skill. The goal for the client is to say and feel, "I am who I think I am; and I think I am a worthwhile person with style. Who you think I am is interesting but is not a basis for my deciding who I am, unless what you have to say really does seem to fit my perceptions of my behavior and actions. Nonetheless, I appreciate your sharing your thoughts and ideas with me."

To reiterate an earlier point, the readiness of the client is in proportion to the perceived benefit for him as well as related to his looking beyond simple self-interest and seeing each family member as benefitting from the client's participation.

The client is doing it for himself but also for the other people in the family. This perspective combines with a realistic appraisal by the client of his abilities, skills, and capacity to function within the family in an effective way. These two components of readiness then combine with the client's excepting responsibility for his participation in the family and participation in the educational approach.

PART TWO

DEVELOPING INTERPERSONAL STYLE

INTRODUCTION

LOOKING AT BEHAVIOR

YOU WILL FIND that people have a strong tendency to initially understand their behavior within their families as generally either a reaction to or an accommodation to the behavior, needs, and interests of others. Children will see themselves reacting to or accommodating to their siblings and/or parents, while parents will see themselves reacting to or accommodating to their children and/or each other. Within the marital dyad, the same reaction/accommodation interpretation applies even when there are no children in the family. To a very significant degree, people believe their behavior and adjustment to be significantly dependent on or contingent on the behavior and adjustment of others in the family. This point especially applies when they are focusing on interpersonal difficulties or problem points.

A central goal of this section is to assist individuals in accepting full responsibility for their behavior and adjustment and to facilitate their thinking of themselves as autonomous, independent, and in charge of their actions and responses.

ACTIVITY 4

MULTIDIMENSIONAL STYLE

WE ARE multidimensional people. This first means that we have a physical dimension that takes in our physical selves, the kinds of things we do and avoid doing, and the ways in which we deal with ourselves as physical/doing people. We have an emotional dimension that has to do with how we manage our emotions and feelings and how we understand and respond to the emotions and feelings of others. We have a moral dimension that has to do with our personal values, what we will do and what we will not do, what we think is okay and not okay, and how we manage ourselves as moral people. We also have a social dimension that has to do with being a friend, relating to other people, being involved in social activities, and other things related to our interpersonal relationships. Our sexual dimension has to do with how we handle ourselves sexually, how we see ourselves as sexual people, how we manage our sexual relationships, and how we treat others and expect to be treated sexually. We are also thinking people and have a cognitive or thinking dimension. This has to do with how we use logic and our intuitions, how we go about solving problems, how we go about trying to understand things around us, and how we use our minds and abilities to learn.

Our way of handling ourselves, what we think is important, and the impression we want to give to others within each of these dimensions go to make up our personal style. Please complete each of the sentences below, making one statement about yourself and your style. Try to make the statement true for you as you really are. You may finish the sentence in anyway that fits you.

1. Physically, I am ____.
2. Emotionally, I am ____.
3. Morally, I am ____.

4. Socially, I am ____.
5. Sexually, I am ____.
6. Cognitively, I am ____.

Check back to be sure that each statement represents a positive statement about you. If not, go back and refinish the statement, making a positive statement about yourself. It is your style you are talking about. Always think about what you have going for you first. There is plenty of time to think about the less flattering points.

Now, BE THE PERSON YOU ARE—WITH STYLE—ALL THE TIME—ON PURPOSE.

DISCUSSION

The above activity facilitates interpersonal skill development in three areas. First, the focusing on the six dimensions helps the client to think in terms of her interpersonal participation in more specific terms than is usually the case for most individuals. They are inclined to think in terms of their behavior without understanding that they project themselves in multiple ways, with each dimension representing who they are as a function of self-perception and who they are in terms of perceptions of others. Consultants will find that some individuals need assistance in looking at themselves physically, emotionally, morally, socially, sexually, and cognitively. Nonetheless, the activity will lead to the client's being more aware of herself and of her presentation to others.

Next, the activity facilitates the client's thinking about the multidimensional styles of other family members. For example, a client might begin to see that one family member acts more based on what is thought about something while another family member acts more on what is felt about it. One family member may think more in terms of the social or interpersonal implications of an incident while another family member thinks more in terms of the emotional implications. The consultant will want to facilitate the use of the activity to highlight these differing ways of understanding family members.

In addition, it may be useful to have the client set up a grid with each family member listed down the left hand side and the six dimensions listed across the top. Each family member can simply be noted by a check mark in the column most applicable to her. In addition, the client could rate each family member on a five-point scale indicating how the family member functions within each of the six dimensions. The five point scale would consist of: 5 equals very strong emphasis, 4 equals strong emphasis, 3 equals medium emphasis, 2 equals weak emphasis, 1 equals very weak emphasis. Once the grid is completed, the consultant may assist the client in thinking about the implications for the family of the completed grid.

Finally, the activity emphasizes the concept of style. Most people will intuitively understand the idea of style, especially if they are asked to note two or three people that they know in or out of the family that, from their point of view, have real style. Importantly, style is here understood as positive and represents the overall effect of self projection to others. Three characteristics of style need emphasis: recognizability, definability, and predictability.

Style is recognizable. It is the general impression or idea of someone that develops and can be understood in terms of the six dimensions. The activity, of course, facilitates the client's recognizing her style but also facilitates recognition of style in others.

Style is definable. As a preliminary activity, the consultant may want to have the client simply list those traits and characteristics of individuals that she finds to be the most positive, most appealing, the most characteristic of real style. This then begins to get the client into the definition mode relative to style. The activity itself assists the client's defining her style in multidimensional terms.

Each of the responses in the activity should be positive, since one's style is a positive projection of self. Also, this positive orientation assists the client in looking at other family members in essentially positive terms. In this sense, the educational process begins maximizing and emphasizing the strengths and positive features within each family member and encourages a positive orientation to specific areas of family life developed in later activities.

Style is predictable. This point is at the essence of the activity. The underlying goal is to encourage the client to understand and take responsibility for her style. This responsibility taking necessarily involves developing and maintaining a consistent and positive self-projection. Predictability of style additionally means that the style of the individual does not change as a function of reactions of others, special circumstances, whether or not the client likes or is comfortable with what is going on at the time, or similarly externally initiated factors.

This point is emphasized by drawing attention to people with what might be thought of as pseudo style. These individuals appear to have style in terms of its recognizability and definability. The lack of predictability, however, shows that they are not taking the personal responsibility to project themselves consistently and with real style, regardless of the situation or circumstances.

Consciously accepting responsibility for self and self-projection—is the intentional or "on purpose" nature of real style. It is not something that comes about naturally, accidently, or circumstantially. Style is a function of conscious self-awareness, self-examination, and intentional positive self-projection in the interest of more effective interpersonal involvement and relationships. It is something one reflects with style, all the time, on purpose.

ACTIVITY 5

GROUP ROLES

WHICH TATOR are you? It is easy to start analyzing ourselves and others in our families and to take what happens personally. A better way to look at what goes on is to understand that people grow into certain roles or styles and are usually just being whomever they are out of habit or just because that is the way their personalities are. They are just being TATORS. If we are able to understand this and accept them for the TATOR they are, we will all be a lot more comfortable.

Using a scale from five to one rate yourself in terms of how frequently you are each of the following TATORS. Five equals almost always, four equals usually, three equals sometimes, two equals seldom, and one equals almost never. Once you have finished for yourself, it will be fun to think about each of the other people in your family and rate each family member in terms of how frequently he/she is a TATOR.

___ 1. Agitator: Agi likes to keep things stirred up, find fault, criticize, and make things seem worse than they really are.

___ 2. Anitator: Ani likes to have the last word, always "gets his/her two cents worth in," and always has an opinion on everything and likes to show others that he/she knows more than everyone else.

___ 3. Commentator: Commen likes to be sure that everyone knows everything that is going on, is in charge of gossip and "tattling," and seems to talk all the time even if no one wants to listen or if everyone already knew about what is being said.

___ 4. Dicktator: Dick likes to take charge, boss everyone around, be the one who makes all the decisions, and generally be in charge of everything whether or not it is his/her business or responsibility.

___ 5. Gravitator: Gravi is pretty much of a "couch potatoe," always hanging around and there when others want a little privacy, and always seems to be too tired to help out, do things, or get out of the way.

___ 6. Hesitator: Hesi can never decide, always waits to see what someone else's opinion is and then uses that one, is very unsure of himself/herself, goes out of the way not to offend anyone or get anyone upset, and thinks that if he/she can please everyone all the time things will be okay.

___ 7. Levitator: Levi thinks he/she is just a little better than everyone else, is sort of above it all most of the time, seems like he/she is looking down the nose at others, and feels pretty much superior to everyone else.

___ 8. Meditator: Medi seems to take forever to do things because he/she has to think everything over very carefully before doing something, never wants to do anything quickly or on the spur of the moment because anything worth doing is worth thinking through carefully, and is usually hard to talk with because everything has to be analyzed and discussed in great detail.

___ 9. Militator: Mili is always on guard and ready to go to war, will argue with anyone about anything anytime, never gives an inch, and is ready to stand his/her ground with anyone who tries to take advantage or confront him/her.

___10. Precipitator: Precipi is one of those TATORS that is able to get other people into arguments and then walk away, say or do things that get others upset and then pretend like he/she is totally innocent, and seems to get things messed up or stirred up without seeming to have started it or without seeming to have been involved.

___11. Spectator: Spec likes to stay on the sidelines and not really get involved, simply watch or listen without really participating, and just stays to himself/herself because that seems like the safest way of just getting by without getting involved.

___12. Facilitator: Facili does not mind being out of alphabetical order because his/her job is to be helpful, to do things for other people, to be there when others need him/her, and to stay away from things that have to do with accepting responsibility, showing leadership, or running the risk of being blamed for what is done or how things turn out.

___13. Baby Sweetator: Baby Sweet is the kind of TATOR that is always happy and cheerful no matter what, is too nice for anyone to get upset with even if he/she does something that they should get upset about, cries or has his/her feelings hurt very easily, and tries to get special treatment just because he/she is so sweet, innocent, and not really responsible for anything that happens that is bad or causes problems for others.

DISCUSSION

The thirteen TATORS and the activity within which they are included represent a way of encouraging the client to look at himself and at others within his family in behavioral terms in relationship to what may be perceived as problematic participation within the family. Typically, individuals will be inclined to infer the existence of negative motivations and complex psychological issues when dealing with family members who are into TATOR roles. At the same time, these individuals will also be inclined to interpret similar behavior on their parts as justified, reasonable, necessary, and free from negative motivation or psychological complexity. The usual approach comes in terms of, "When I am a TATOR I am functioning in the best interest of the family; but when you are a TATOR you are being a 'pain in the neck.' "

The idea of the activity is to move away from these types of interpretations and toward understanding the behavior and participation of each family member as simply reflecting their individual and idiosyncratic style. In addition, the activity gives the client new names or labels for certain behaviors or participation styles. This is a positive step since the names or labels given to behavior or participation do, themselves, effect the behavior and reflect a general attitude toward the individual and less directly toward the family as a system. The more neutral or acceptable the label, the more neutral or acceptable the attitude and the easier it is for each family member to understand and relate to other family members.

In addition to the general value of the activity, the client also benefits from looking at his intrafamily behavior in terms of tendencies he may have to take on somewhat stereotypic roles or behavior patterns. Most individuals will find it easiest to decrease TATOR behavior in those areas where such behavior is reflected less often, while increasing their ability to deal nonreactively with family members for whom TATOR behavior is more frequent. More specifically, it will be easiest for individuals to decrease behavior in which they become involved on a seldom or almost never basis. Alternatively, they will be best able to develop a strategy for relating to and responding to TATOR behavior in others when that type of behavior is the normal or usual pattern seen in another family member. Generally, it is easier to develop a strategy for responding to the behavior of others when that behavior is reasonably frequent and predictable. More difficulty arises when such behavior is less predictable, more occasional, and more likely to come up on an unexpectedly spontaneous basis.

Recognition of particular problematic behavior is the key to reducing or modifying that behavior. Education comes through seeing how involvement and the TATOR role is perceived by and interpreted by others. The brief descriptor in the activity lets the individual see how others perceive him when he is a TATOR. Consultation then needs to focus on alternative ways of relating and interacting. The next activity will be especially useful in this respect. For example, being assertive, decisive, and considerate—as discussed in the next activity—are very useful alternatives to being a DICKTATOR.

When learning to respond to TATORS, the client will be best served by techniques and strategies that understand and refuse participation in "the game." In the remainder of this discussion, focus will be on the game, how not to get "hooked" into the game, and productive alternatives to being a TATOR.

The AGITATORS game is based on focusing on the negative side of people and situations, emphasizing those negatives or problematic pieces, and tempting others to become defensive or negatively reactive. If another family member does become defensive or negatively reactive, the AGITATOR has "won" the game by being validated as someone with enough power, control, and influence in the family to get others upset and negatively interacting. Importantly, this is simply a style that develops as the result of its having been reinforced over time, a history of the game's resulting in the agitator's winning. The agitator is reluctant to give up the game since it provides for him a position of power, control, influence, and reinforcement within the family.

The key to avoiding being hooked by the agitator is to anticipate his behavior. It is predictable that he will criticize, make things seem worse than they really are, and try to keep things stirred up. Through one's behavior and active interaction, the first step is to simply to refuse to react to the negativism. Simply sit quietly and say nothing. Next, it is important to convey to the agitator an understanding of the game. "Your usual style is to be an agitator. This is true when there are problems but is also true when there really are no problems. Also, you make a sport out of criticizing and finding fault. You are an AGITATOR. I am simply not going to react to you any more. Now that I know how the game works, I refuse to play." The alternative for the agitator is to move to a position where he is more positive, fair, and playful, spending less time and energy being negative and agitative.

The ANITATOR game develops for individuals in much the same way as the AGITATOR game. The payoff or win comes through perceiving one's self as "one up" or somewhat superior to others. For the anitator, this position in the family is important as a way of developing and maintaining his self-esteem and self-confidence. If other family members respond by arguing, trying to get in the last word themselves, or by refusing to let the anitator "butt in" or impose himself into the conversation, the anitator will feel rebuffed and will probably pout. This behavior then becomes the second level of the game, designed to get others to apologize or to try to coax the anitator back into anitating behavior. However the process proceeds, the anitator is in control.

The key to not getting hooked by the anitator is to first directly confront the anitator about his behavior. Say, "You are an ANITATOR. You always seem to have to have the last word, have to get your two cents worth in whether it is wanted or not, and always act like you know more than everyone else. This type of behavior causes me to have negative feelings toward you and makes it very difficult for me to relate to you. It will surely be nice when you no longer feel like you have to play 'one up' with everyone all the time. In the meantime, I am simply not going to listen when you have to get in the last word or try to put your two cents worth in when it is not wanted or are criticizing people or putting people down."

The key here is to stop. No matter what the anitator says next, do not get hooked again. Also, simply ignore the anitator if he chooses to pout and withdraw as a result of being confronted by his behavior. The anitator needs to learn to be a better listener, more patient, and more tolerant of others. Also, he needs to learn to be more considerate of others and their needs for attention, recognition, acceptance, and affirmation.

The COMMENTATOR plays a similar but slightly different game. The win comes for the commentator through constant interaction and attention seeking. He has not developed alternative interpersonal and intrafamily skills that assure interaction, attention, and feedback from others and has learned to assure these through being a commentator. His behavior has the effect of getting others into arguments and states of conflicts through tattling and gossiping which result in increased interaction and tension in which commentator vicariously participates but for which he is not held responsible.

The first step to avoid being hooked is to confront the commentator in a manner similar to that used with the anitator. Let him know that you are aware of the game, do not like it, and are not going to play anymore. Let him know when you are interested in listening and when you are not, subject matter that is of interest to you and that which is not, and be sure not to react negatively to or interact negatively with other family members based on information you have received from the commentator. He needs to learn to be more relaxed, more loyal to members of the family, and more dependable in terms of the accuracy and importance of the information he conveys. Also, let him know that you simply assume that he is saying the same types of things to other family members about you as is being said to you about them. The commentator's game can get vicious; so it is very important that other family members unanimously refuse to play.

As with all family TATORS, the adults in the family must take primary responsibility for dealing with the family TATORS, although older children and teens may actively participate in the process to the extent that participation is permitted by the adult DICKTATOR if there is one in the family. Remember that children are not on a par with adults in terms of their ability or position when trying to deal in healthy and constructive ways with older TATORS in the family. They may have little alternative to playing the game, although consultation directed specifically to children can help them develop the techniques and strategies that minimize the negative effects of interacting with older TATORS, including adult game players.

The DICKTATOR'S game is straightforward. He directly exercises power, control, and influence which are the underlying motivators of all TATOR game players. The win comes through controlling, being in charge, and holding more power than other members of the family. If the client is in the position to refuse to capitulate to the will and direction of the dicktator, doing so on a reasonable and consistent basis is the best way to respond to the DICKTATOR'S game.

When the dicktator is into his role, simply stop to think about whether or not the dicktator's advice is sound, direction is correct, or ideas are worth further consideration. If so, let the dicktator know that, after due consideration, his dictates are being followed. This step by itself lets the dicktator know that he is not in charge, is not the boss. By the same token, it is important to refuse to go along or follow the dictate, if doing so does not seem reasonable, appropriate, or productive. This moderated, responsible approach will gradually reduce the authority and dictatorial behavior of the dicktator.

One must avoid a simple negative reaction in terms of routinely refusing to cooperate, refusing to follow directives, refusing to listen to the dicktator's point of view. Blind refusual is as counterproductive as blind capitulation and represents an alternative way of playing the game, but still constitutes game playing. Directly confronting the dicktator about his behavior is seldom useful but is probably in the interest of healthy and assertive acceptance of personal responsibility. The dicktator needs to gradually become more accepting, more aware of those things that do and do not contribute to his attractiveness to other family members, more flexible, and more supportive of other family members. The key to this is becoming more tolerant of the interests, preferences, and idiosyncratic styles of other members of the family.

The GRAVITATOR plays a game noticeably different from those discussed to this point. The games considered thus far have an active, doing quality about them. GRAVITATOR'S game is more passive and considerably more subtle. He wins by intruding into the activities of others, forcing other people to accommodate to him, and doing all of this in a way that avoids his having to put forth effort and energy, take responsibility, or show any significant degree of initiative. Others find this behavior annoying, frustrating, and see it as an imposition; but the hook is in terms of their feeling guilty if they confront gravitator, demand their space, or insist that gravitator do his share. It is as if they were making demands on an individual who is unable to respond or comply. Pushing would feel a little bit like victimizing the victim. The result is that they expect very little from gravitator, respond to what come to be seen as his demands, and allow gravitator to have considerably more than his fair share of family space, energy, and socioemotional tolerance.

The key in dealing with gravitator is to understand that it is a game that he plays. Other family members need to be more assertive and responsible in terms of insisting on their rights and on gravitator's carrying his share of the load. On the one hand, other family members simply ignore gravitator's behavior while on the other hand refusing to respond to his direct and indirect needs that usually come in the form of pleas and weak request. Say to gravitator, "I need my space or privacy and will appreciate your laying around some place else." Also one might say, "I am no longer going to be helpful to you and respond to your needs and interests unless doing so becomes a reciprocal arrangement." Gravitator needs to become more helpful, more actively involved in the family, more responsible, a more dependable participant in the family system, and considerably more energetic both at a personal and family system level.

Within the family game arena, HESITATOR plays a game with many similarities to that of GRAVITATOR. Although hesitator brings more energy to the family system, he takes a very passive approach to family activities and involvements. It is a no lose game. If problems are solved, decisions prove to be useful, and things go along smoothly, hesitator may share in the credit since he agreed to and supported what happened. Alternatively, if things do not go smoothly, do not work out well, hesitator is free from responsibility since he can always plead having been uneasy with the decision or plan to begin with and can note that he only reluctantly went along. Either way, hesitator wins.

Other family members will need to become more assertive with hesitator, confront him about the game, whenever possible avoid making decisions or taking positions until hesitator has committed himself, and simply refuse to acknowledge the win. "Things worked out alright but you had nothing to do with that. It is not true that you supported or went along with the decision. If you do not take active responsibility at the beginning, you get no credit at the end. By the same token, when things do not work out, you are as responsible for that as anyone else. Your refusal to actively participate does not in any way diminish your responsibility within the family." Hesitator must learn to be more responsible, more assertive, more involved, and more active within family life, good times, bad times, and all.

As was true with the HESITATOR, the LEVITATOR plays a game very similar to the GRAVITATOR. The twist comes in terms of levitator's remaining detached and uninvolved from what seems to be a sense of superiority. Hesitator seems to reflect more a sense of inferiority, with levitator being at the opposite end of the same illusory range. The range is an illusion because it simply represents somewhat different ways of avoiding involvement, responsibility, and active participation within the family system.

The win for levitator comes either in terms of other's capitulating or their becoming frustrated and reactive. In either event, the ideas, interests, and feelings of other family members may simply be discounted.

Levitator needs to be called on the game, needs to learn that others will not capitulate or accept their implied inferiority, and will only deal with him as an equal, active participant within the family system. Levitator needs to learn to become more attractive to other family members in social and emotional terms, to be more considerate of the feelings and interests of others, and to be more supportive of the needs and interests of others.

MEDITATOR plays a game very similar to that of the HESITATOR but brings considerably more energy and activity to the game. Meditator will accept responsibility for decisions, plans, and other activities but will only do so if there is almost complete certainty relative to the outcome. The win comes through only taking responsibility for those things that are nearly certain and thus being guaranteed of a positive outcome when he does take responsibility. The rest of the time, he can hold others accountable for problematic outcomes with the added benefit of being able to say, "I warned you or I told you so." Meditator is not refusing to participate and shows no reluctance to participate.

The hook for others comes in terms of running the risk of being held responsible when there are problems or when things do not work out well. They want to avoid being the goat and thus play meditator's game. The key to avoiding being hooked into the game is to understand two basic concepts. First, consider the law of probability. Although meditator will approach 100 percent in terms of decisions and plans that work out, other family members will come close to that same level based on their experience, judgement, and general good sense. The meditator's track record will not be much better than that of other family members over time. Second, playing the meditator's game results in many missed opportunities, plans that never got off the ground, and activities that never happened. Not playing the game results in a lot more positive outcomes for the family with only a slight increase in problematic outcomes. The small risk is well worth the significant payoff over time. Meditator needs to learn to be more decisive, more flexible, more playful, and more relaxed about the ups and downs of life within the family system.

MILITATOR plays a game similar to that played by DICKTATOR. Whereas the dicktator is intent on exercising power, control, and influence by making all of the decisions and telling everyone what to do, the militator similarly exercises power, control, and influence by not letting anyone in the family exercise power, control, or influence over him, tell him what to do.

For the militator, the win comes through always having control, always having the upper hand, by never letting anyone put one over on him or exercise control in relationship to him. The key to dealing with militator is to confront without arguing. Anytime militator becomes argumentative or confrontive, simply say, "I appreciate your sharing your point of view and will take it into consideration." Militator will likely try to continue confronting or arguing. It is then appropriate to say, "You simply like to be confrontive for confrontation's sake, like to argue for the sake of arguing. I have told you that I appreciate your sharing your point of view and will take it into consideration. I have no more to say on this particular subject." Stick to this decision and do not discuss the topic any further with militator. He needs to learn to be more accepting of other family members and of their feelings and ideas, to be more assertive without becoming confrontive or argumentative, to be more considerate of the needs and interests of others, to be more flexible, to be more gentle, and to be more patient and playful with others.

PRECIPITATOR plays a game similar to that played by the MILITATOR; but the precipitator plays it more indirectly and is able to get others to do his bidding. The win comes through getting others upset and into conflict without needing to get upset or participate in the conflict in any direct way. The payoff is vicarious and indirect.

The strategy for dealing with the precipitator is somewhat unlike that used with other TATORS. Here, the key is for all other family members to talk with each other about the precipitator's game, how they are getting hooked in, and how the win works for precipitator. Other family members may then simply refuse to react, come to the bait, or become upset with each other as a result of what precipitator says or does. In addition, it may be useful for the family as a group to sit down, talk with the precipitator about his game, and share with him how it is going to be dealt with by other members of the family. The precipitator needs to learn to be more actively involved in family life, to maintain a more positive orientation to each member of the family, and to accept considerably more responsibility for his behavior and participation within the family.

The SPECTATOR game within the family has qualities similar to the games of the GRAVITATOR and the HESITATOR. However, spectator's game is much more passive and indirect. In fact, spectator is simply refusing to be an active part of the family. The win comes through consciously being isolated, uninvolved, detached, and apart from other family members. The payoff is in safety, an absence of responsibility;

and although spectator does not enjoy the benefits of family participation, neither does he have to deal with the tensions, conflicts, problems, and difficulties that come up from time to time.

Simply ignoring spectator only serves to perpetuate his game. Gentle confrontation is in order combined with increased acceptance of spectator, increased assertiveness with him, more consistency when dealing with him, a little more energy brought to relationships with him, and increased spontaneity within relationships with spectator. He needs to learn to be more assertive, more attractive to other members of the family, more energetic in terms of family participation, more giving in social and emotional terms, more playful and more responsible in terms of the value of and need for his active participation in the family.

The family FACILITATOR plays an interesting and somewhat unusual game. The main difficulty in spotting the game comes in terms of the apparent value or desirability of playing facilitator's game. He is helpful, will do almost anything for anyone, and is always there when others need him. These desirable qualities mask or hide the underlying game. The dual win comes first in terms of having others feel obligated to facilitator. They owe him for past favors. The apparently freely given favors and services are the hook. The underlying aspect of the win comes in terms of facilitator's not needing to accept responsibility, make decisions, show leadership, or deal with his fair share of the give and take within family life. Even if these negatives are upsetting or irritating to others, they have difficulty dealing with facilitator about them since they feel obligated as a function of past favors and as a function of favors and services anticipated in the future. The result is that facilitator is left free from sanction or criticism.

The key to dealing with facilitator comes in terms of simply refusing to accept favors or services which one could get along without or reasonably provide for himself. In addition, it is equally important to avoid feeling that one should "pay back" the facilitator by not holding him responsible for family involvement and participation. He might say, "Why do you treat me this way after all I have done for you?" An appropriate response would be, "I relate to you and deal with you in what I believe to be reasonable and fair ways of relating to and dealing with members of our family. All you have done is indicative of the way you choose to relate to and deal with the rest of us. In our family, we are helpful to each other and also hold each other accountable for and responsible for appropriate participation." Facilitator needs to learn to be more personally accountable, more responsible, more dependable during times of difficulty or stress, and more open and up front about his motivations and interest.

BABY SWEETATOR concludes the discussion about games played within families. His game is similar to that of the FACILITATOR, although the hook is in terms of personality as opposed to doing favors and providing services for others. The game is to be and remain highly attractive to other family members in physical, emotional, and social terms and to emphasize positive interpersonal gain within relationships. Being involved with someone who reflects these characteristics is the first level of the hook and is a nice and pleasant experience for everyone else. The second level of the hook comes in terms of Baby Sweetator's getting upset, crying, and implying through his behavior that others are being insensitive, inconsiderate, unjustifiably harsh, and unappreciative. The win comes, of course, through avoiding responsibility, criticism and negative interaction with others, and being held accountable for his behavior in both positive and negative terms.

Dealing with baby sweetator is handled the same way as was seen with the FACILITATOR. Basically, one says, "You're nice, a lot of fun, and very pleasant to be around most of the time. Nonetheless, this does not excuse you from responsibility, accountability, or full participation in the family." One then deals with baby sweetator in a straightforward, reasonably objective manner, enjoying the positive aspects of the relationship and dealing directly with the more negative or problematic aspects of the relationships. Baby Sweetator needs to learn to be more consistent, more dependable, more helpful, more socially and emotionally honest, and more responsible in terms of his overall participation within the family.

ACTIVITY 6

ELEMENTS OF POSITIVE INTERPERSONAL STYLE

BELOW ARE thirty words that describe interpersonal traits, attitudes, or characteristics that are found in effective relationships. Your being a person with style who is good at relationships depends on how often these traits and characteristics are present in your relationships. Using a scale from five to one, rate yourself in terms of how often these traits and characteristics are present for you in your relationships with your family members. Five equals almost always, four equals usually, three equals sometimes, two equals seldom, and one equals almost never.

Using one word at a time and rating yourself on each item, think in terms of a statement that says, "In my relationships with people in my family, I am ___________." Fill in the blank with each of the thirty words below and then rate yourself in terms of the thirty statements.

___ 1. Accepting
___ 2. Affectionate
___ 3. Ambitious
___ 4. Assertive
___ 5. Attractive
___ 6. Considerate
___ 7. Consistent
___ 8. Dependable
___ 9. Decisive
___10. Energetic
___11. Fair
___12. Flexible
___13. Gentle
___14. Giving
___15. Hardworking
___16. Helpful
___17. Honest
___18. Involved
___19. Loyal
___20. Moral
___21. Open
___22. Patient
___23. Playful
___24. Positive
___25. Predictable
___26. Relaxed
___27. Responsible
___28. Spontaneous
___29. Supportive
___30. Tolerant

DISCUSSION

(Note) As a general guideline, the client may wish to add together her thirty numerical responses. This will result in a total interpersonal effectiveness score of from thirty to one hundred fifty. That total may then be divided by thirty resulting in a number from 1.0 to 5.0. This represents, for the client, her interpersonal effectiveness score. Generally, family members who maintain interpersonal effectiveness score of 4.0 or higher are relating well within their families. When there are difficulties, it may be useful for the client to focus on increasing those characteristics that are already at a 3.0 or 4.0 level, with the idea being that it is easier to do more of what you are already doing reasonably well. Over time, focus can be developed in terms of the more problematic characteristics. The exercise is also useful in terms of having the client rate other members of her family and discussing these perceptions with the consultant and with the other family members.

Traditionally, focus on interpersonal relationships has been in terms of problems, difficulties, and explanations as to why things are not working. This activity addresses the same type of issue in a positive direction asking why things are working, why things are going well. What is found is that interpersonally effective individuals develop and maintain relationships that reflect an individualized mix of the 30 traits and characteristics in the activity. If one wants to be more interpersonally effective, the key is to simply maximize the extent to which these traits and characteristics are reflected in her relationships.

Increasing a particular trait or characteristic may be achieved by either directly increasing the trait or characteristic on the one hand or decreasing the alternative or opposite behavior on the other hand. For example, one may focus on the positive traits and characteristics of a specific family member. Focusing attention on these positives will have the effect of increasing the general acceptance of that family member. Alternatively, the opposite of acceptance is rejection or indifference. Increased acceptance will be achieved if rejection is decreased and indifference is exchanged for interest and involvement. The consultant may facilitate focus on the specific behavioral correlates involved in either approach to increasing acceptance.

Being more affectionate needs to be understood in physical, emotional, and social terms. At a physical level, the client may need instruction in touching, holding, and caressing in more gentle and affectionate ways. In addition, verbal tone and content along with facial expression will need attention. At an emotional level, the need is for increased positive emotion, expression of pleasure and satisfaction with the other person, and an increased calm, relaxed approach to the other family member. At the social level, more spontaneous, positive interaction is needed with the content of that interaction emphasizing activities and involvements that the other family member values and enjoys.

Increasing the level of ambition in a client is difficult but straight forward. The alternative perception is of the client as being lazy. The client will need to bring more energy to her activities and family involvements, will need to actively participate more, and will need to more clearly function in the interest of the well being and welfare of the family in physical, emotional, and social terms.

Assertiveness training is explored in great detail in both the popular and professional literature. Basically, it operates in two ways. First, assertiveness falls between passivity and aggression. The passive client needs to learn to stick up for herself, press her point of view, and more spontaneously share her thoughts and ideas. The aggressive client must learn to tone down and modulate her physical, emotional, and social aggression in ways that make her more attractive and acceptable to other family members. The key to either strategy is staying more relaxed, taking more responsibility for individual participation, and developing specific physical, verbal, emotional, and social techniques through which one can be an equal and effective participant within the family. The key to this is assuring that the client avoids playing "games" as discussed in the last activity. Honest, congruent, responsible participation within the family will, by itself, gradually lead to a more appropriately assertive style of family participation.

Increasing attractiveness comes primarily through understanding that "attractiveness" represents the extent to which other members of the family are attracted to the client. People are attracted to each other for different reasons in different ways. Importantly, this attractiveness mix includes physical characteristics but also includes behavioral characteristics such as language, helpfulness, personal appearance, and other aspects of the physical/doing dimension as discussed in relationship to other activities. One way to get at this is to simply ask other family members what kinds of things they find attractive within the physical/doing dimension. Attractiveness also includes emotional attractiveness in terms of one's moods, general emotional positiveness, and the way one manages her emotions. Attractiveness goes on to include moral/spiritual attractiveness, social/interpersonal attractiveness, sexual/sensual attractiveness, and intellectual/cognitive attractiveness. Real attractiveness is seldom limited to one or two areas and virtually never depends more on superficial qualities than on more general characteristics of the individual. Of course, it is also important to decrease those factors that others find unattractive.

Considerateness is a similar characteristic and involves taking the other person into consideration. This includes consideration for their physical needs and interests, need for privacy and physical space, need for physical noninterference with their person or possessions, and a general consideration of them as physical/doing people. The other dimensions within the multidimensional functioning of individuals also become focal areas for consideration. Perhaps easily overlooked is the need to be considerate of the values and beliefs of others and the need to be considerate of their individual styles related to intellectual and cognitive functioning. In addition, people want to have their feelings taken into consideration and their social styles understood and considered. Generally, each person in the family needs to know that each of the other people in the family takes her into consideration fully, sensitively, and caringly.

The multidimensionality of consistency is similar to that seen with characteristics already discussed. It is also closely aligned with dependability in terms of interpersonal style and interpersonal effectiveness. Both consistency and dependability can be understood in terms of physical/doing behavior and activities, following through with commitments and agreements, and being there when others need someone to be there for them. Importantly, both also have a feeling/emotional dimension. Emotional consistency and dependability are perhaps as important as physical/behavioral consistency and dependability. The same holds for social consistency and dependability as one is involved in family activities, relates to other family members, and functions as part of the family's social environment.

All of these characteristics require the individual to bring enough energy to family participation to reflect the characteristics with style, all the time, on purpose. This applies to physical energy and also applies to emotional and social energy.

Fairness and flexibility are additional characteristics of the interpersonally effective individual. Both are closely linked to consideration and convey a fairly simple approach to other family members. "I will deal with you fairly, responding to your needs, interests, rights, and responsibilities. If necessary, I will adjust my thinking, behavior, and attitudes to develop an appropriate congruence with yours. This means that along with being fair, I will also relate to you in a flexible way that allows each of us to be comfortable with ourselves and with each other."

Gentleness may, in fact, be one of the more important interpersonal elements to cultivate for most individuals experiencing interpersonal difficulty within the family. At a system level, most families would function much better if each family member would simply increase the level of gentleness she brings to family relationships. Of course, gentleness is multidimensional as are the other traits and characteristics. This then includes emotional gentleness and a gentle approach to social involvement and participation as well as physical gentleness. The consultant will find that people frequently need specific instruction in being more physically gentle but also in being more emotionally gentle with each other.

Being helpful and hardworking are fairly straightforward ideas related to doing things that are useful for other family members and for the family as a whole. Importantly, though, helpfulness and being hardworking also extend to the emotional and social environment of the family. Positive social and emotional environments within the family do not necessarily occur naturally or spontaneously. They are a result of effort and the investment of time and energy, requiring skill and sensitivity. Essential here is a high level of physical, emotional, and social involvement in the family and the life of the family.

Honesty, loyalty, and a high priority given to personal morality give emphasis to the values and beliefs that underlie and support the family system. Collectively they may be thought of as representing the individual culture of a family and represent the base on which all other aspects of family life and involvements rest. They, of course, relate to the actions of individual family members and to how family members relate to each other verbally. In addition, though, honesty, loyalty, and morality also underlie the emotional and social environments within the family. Focusing specifically on loyalty, it should be understood that loyalty is a manifestation of the morality and fundamental honesty of the family and its members. At a basic level, loyalty is the commitment to "hang in there" with each other in positive and supportive ways. A commitment to morality and honesty drive loyalty and become the underlying reason for family members being loyal to each other.

Openness is very closely related to honesty and thus to loyalty and morality within the family system. Developing emotional and intellectual openness is the key and represents an honest, congruent approach to relating to and participating with others. It has to do with not masking, disguising or covering up feelings on the one hand and with not over expressing feelings and emotions on the other hand. Similarly, it has to do with candidly and straightforwardly expressing one's thoughts, views, and ideas without making them seem stronger or more fixed than they really are. Openness is, perhaps, at the opposite end of interpersonal styles from games. Everything is out on the table where one can see it, deal with it, and respond to it. It is not possible to fully and congruently deal with each other within the family unless each member is willing and able to develop a high level of openness with other members of the family.

Patience, playfulness, and positiveness combine with being relaxed and predictable to develop a level of receptivity and safety for others that allows them to seek out the individual and relate to her in an easy and pleasurable manner. An important part of interpersonal effectiveness has to do with not only how the individual relates to others but also how easy and facilitated it is for others to relate to her. Patience generally conveys a willingness to allow the other person to be who she is and to relate in her own time and on her own terms. The other person does not develop a sense of demand or expectation within the relationship. The positive opportunity and feedback the other person receives encourages further relating and involvement. When all of this takes place within a playful, "enjoying each other" relationship the interpersonally effective individual becomes a source of comfort, fun, and escape from the tensions and turmoils outside of the relationship and outside of the family.

Essential to these and other interpersonally effective characteristics is a lack of anxiety, tension, and turmoil. To achieve this, the individual needs to learn to consciously and intentionally stay reasonably calm, reasonably slowed-down, and reasonably free from anxiety and tension. Here the consultant may be of specific assistance in terms of teaching breathing and other relaxation exercises, such as, self-hypnosis and focused relaxation, or guided imagery. The consultant may also want to interest the client in some of the relaxation activities found in the study of yoga. The progression usually follows from relaxing one's respiration and muscles to mental focus or imagery leading to the relaxation of the mind and rushing thoughts. These two steps in turn lead to emotional relaxation and a sense of calmness or equanimity. For clients who have a tendency toward excess anxiety or tension, the consultant may want to start with the relaxation element as a prerequisite to effective work in developing the other positive traits and characteristics.

All of the traits and characteristics discussed to this point begin to mix and combine to develop the interpersonal presentation or projection of the individual to other family members and to develop the interpersonal environment within which others can comfortably relate and interact. The individual will relate with style, all the time, on purpose, reflecting a high degree of consistency and predictability.

Predictability in particular becomes an additional central factor in relationship to being responsible and being tolerant. The latter let people know how they will be dealt with while predictability lets them know that tolerance and dependability are something they can count on and at times can simply take for granted. It is sufficient to note that responsibility not only applies to physical/doing behavior and action but also applies to being emotionally responsible, morally responsible, socially responsible, sexually responsible, and intellectually responsible.

An important part of being responsible involves being tolerant. It is an attitude that is conveyed making it clear that no one is expected to be perfect, expected to do all things correctly at all times. In addition, it conveys an acceptance of others that lets them know that it is okay for them to be who they are without criticism or ridicule.

As can be seen by this point, spontaneity is, then, more than being verbally or socially spontaneous. When something is spontaneous, it occurs without any obvious or external cause or stimulus. It happens simply as a function of the situation, the circumstances, or the general environmental mix present at the time. Family members who are ambitious, assertive, consistent, dependable, decisive, energetic, helpful, involved, open, and responsible in physical, emotional, and social terms will be spontaneous as a part of their effective family participation. Alternatively, individuals who are not relating physically, emotionally, and socially in spontaneous ways need to first understand the extent to which they are also not manifesting other positive and effective traits and characteristics. This insight usually leads to increased spontaneity, especially if the consultant will take a coaching role with the individual in terms of teaching and encouraging relative to spontaneous behavior and opportunities for spontaneity.

ACTIVITY 7

INTERPERSONAL STYLE TYPE

THE CHART below is for your use in determining the usual personal interpersonal style type with which you are most comfortable for yourself. Your usual style falls into one of the four quadrants of the chart below. As you will see, each quadrant contains two representatives from the TATORS and five characteristics from the Interpersonal Elements. Your task is to choose the combination with which you are most comfortable and with which you most identify personally. Once you have chosen the combination that best describes you, that quadrant can then be seen as an approximate description of your style, your way of relating within your family.

You will tend to experience most difficulties with those family members whose styles are best described by the quadrant diagonal from yours. You will have the next level of difficulty with those family members whose styles are best characterized as falling in the same quadrant as yours. The least difficulty will be experienced with family members whose styles are best characterized by the quadrants adjacent to yours.

At the bottom of each quadrant is a short phrase that characterizes the four styles. "Street Fighters" will have the least difficulty with "Cheerleaders" and "Pacifiers." Street Fighters will have more difficulty with other Street Fighters but will experience the highest difficulty trying to deal with "Unanimity Seekers."

Once you have located your style, determine the styles of other family members. When you are having difficulties, do not take it personally. Remember that it is just a matter of style. Things will go better with dictators if you encourage them to be assertive and give them more opportunities to be decisive. Be very selective about those points at which you choose to be confrontive, insist on your rights, or have to have things your way. The idea is not to "roll over and play dead." The idea is to find opportunities for the dictator to be decisive, assertive, spontaneous, energetic, and flexible, with ample opportunity for him/her to feel like he/she won the streetfight. Use the same approach for improving relationships when you are having difficulties with family members who reflect styles from any of the other three quadrants. As a trade-off, encourage them to create opportunities for you to exercise your style more freely and purposefully.

Facilitator/Agitator	**Dictator/Militator**
Helpful Loyal Responsible Dependable Consistent (Pacifier)	Decisive Assertive Spontaneous Energetic Flexible (Street Fighter)
Gravitator/Commentator	**Levitator/Precipitator**
Playful Gentle Open Patient Accepting (Unanimity Seeker)	Involved Positive Relaxed Attractive Supportive (Cheer Leader)

DISCUSSION

This activity begins to consolidate the skills and insights developed through the development of multidimensional style, understanding of group roles, and consideration of the elements of interpersonally effective relationships. Most clients will be comfortable with the forced choice nature of the activity, although some will not. For those individuals, the consultant will need to emphasize the concept of approximation in relationship to the style type and encourage the individual to pick that quadrant that most approximates his style. For a few individuals, it will become clear that they do not reflect any consistent style and spend significant portions of their family energy moving from quadrant to quadrant in terms of style and self-projection. These individuals may be thought of as chameleons or style switchers. The major problem they are experiencing is a significant lack of consistency and predictability. They are, rather, simply trying to accommodate to the needs, whims, and projections of others. This by itself becomes a focus for consultation.

For most individuals who are old enough and reflect enough conceptual development, however, identifying with one of the quadrants will be something they are able to do rather quickly and spontaneously. At the individual level, it is important for the consultant to focus in terms of the extent to which the individual interpersonal style of the client manifests itself as a game as discussed in an earlier activity. Assuming that the client functions in a relatively game free manner, the consultant may encourage an expansion of the perspective from which the activity is viewed.

At a family level, identification of the styles of each family member may be accomplished in two ways. First, the individual client may simply indicate where he thinks each family member belongs in the grid. If two or more family members are participating in the process, they may discuss and try to involve themselves in group decision making relative to the appropriate assignment of each family member. At those points where there is disagreement, sharing perceptions of each other will, itself, be a useful intrafamily process. In addition, the observations of the consultant add an outside perspective to the family discussion.

Importantly, assignment of a family member to one of the quadrants does not represent a value judgement. Being in one quadrant is not better or worse than being in another. The key is simply recognizing and owning one's personal interpersonal style.

Focusing on the pacifiers, it is important to see that their being helpful, loyal, responsible, dependable, and consistent adds a level of stability and cooperation within the family that is a very positive, systemic factor. Their orientation to pacifying has the effect of minimizing conflict and tension and increases the ability of the family to get along and get things done on a day to day basis.

Alternatively, the orientation toward pacifying works against their accepting personal responsibility at times and represents a somewhat shortsighted orientation to problems, difficulties, and significant family issues.

The street fighter's inclination to be decisive, assertive, spontaneous, energetic, and flexible has the effect of moving family processes and activities along. Decisions are made, points of view are expressed, participation occurs as a function of the situation or circumstances, energy is high, and the family is able to change directions, change plans, and respond to what is going on at the moment. Alternatively, the street fighter may be somewhat inconsiderate of the needs and interest of others, may somewhat overwhelm or overpower other members of the family, and may be seen as not able to stick to his ideas, convictions, beliefs, or feelings. The predominate impression may be of an insensitive, self-serving approach to family life.

The gravitator's orientation to unanimity seeking is furthered through his playful, gentle, open, patient, accepting approach to other members of the family. Each member of the family feels acknowledged, understood, and important. The positive effect is a comfortable and safe environment for all. Alternatively, the unanimity seeker may be viewed as not really understanding the significance or seriousness of problems or difficulties, not being able to be tough and make the hard decisions when that is necessary, unnecessarily gullible, and unable to protect his interests or those of the family.

The cheerleader's being involved, positive, relaxed, attractive, and supportive gives him a special place in the family. He is seen as invested in and committed to the life of the family, is always able to see the brighter side of things, is someone to whom others are drawn, and represents a source of continuing encouragement and affirmation. Alternatively, he may be viewed as someone who does not really understand the significance or seriousness of what is happening, as someone who's laid back and calm approach represents a lack of sincerity and caring, and as someone who thinks whatever anyone does or whatever is happening is alright. The effect is an impression of superficiality and insensitivity.

Each quadrant represents a somewhat habitual and natural style and is the style one would tend to project at points of increased stress, conflict, and tension. At these points, a somewhat stereotypic style becomes somewhat counterproductive and may interfere with the smooth functioning of the family system. The key through the educational process is for individuals to recognize those points at which there is increased stress or tension and make some adjustment in or accommodation of style to increase interpersonal congruence and compatibility.

How is this done? The idea is uncomplicated but not always easy. The client looks at the specific situation and pattern of interaction and determines where each individual is functioning at the time. He then adjusts his style toward the quadrant that would result in the best fit while still serving the short and long term interest of the family system. For example, dictators move more in the facilitator direction or in the levitator direction, using the elements in the quadrant to which they are moving as guides or behavioral mandates in reference to how to best reflect more of that style. This might mean that the dictator consciously becomes more helpful or more positive, depending on whether he is moving toward the facilitator quadrant or the levitator quadrant.

Although people will find it nearly impossible to modify their styles toward the quadrant diagonal from theirs, they will usually have little difficulty modifying in the direction of a quadrant adjacent to theirs. The result is that style is not rigid and unresponsive to people and situations. It is, rather, both responsive to and sensitive to other family members and specific situations. This ability to appropriately modify style in turn becomes part of the style of the individual. He is and is seen as an individual who is sensitive, reasonably accommodating, and orientated to both his interest and the special needs and interest of other family members and of the family as a system.

ACTIVITY 8

THE PSYCHOLOGY OF SHARKS AND SEALS

THIS ACTIVITY enables you to look at your interpersonal style and at your style in relationship to the styles of others. You may find the activity most helpful if you first complete the activity and then read the discussion that follows. Once you have completed the discussion, return to the activity and reconsider your responses. Also, this will be a good time to consider your style in relationship to the styles of others.

Here focus is on your basic nature. It is important to get in touch with who you really are and to avoid responding in terms of how you would like to be or how you would like to be seen by others. In each of the five sets below, consider the descriptions of each personality type, get in touch with who you really are, and then circle either "A" or "B," depending on which one most closely parallels your nature. It may help to think in terms of how you would respond or react during times of stress or tension. It is at these times when one's real nature tends to come to the surface.

1-A: SHARKS Sharks are involved and decisive. They are very much into being individuals who are not part of the group and who definitely operate in their own interest. Being involved takes the form of being extremely alert, aware of what is going on, and prepared to act quickly and efficiently. Decisiveness is a major characteristic, with sharks being able to make a decision and act on it without hesitation or second guessing.

B: SEALS Seals are helpful and playful. They are definitely part of the group and social participation is a high priority for them. They like being helpful, doing things for and with others, and making things work out well for everyone. They also have an ability to be helpful in a fun way, with playfulness being one of their primary characteristics.

2-A: LIONS Lions are assertive and positive. They loudly make their presence known and are immediately recognized and are always attended to. Their assertiveness serves them well in terms of furthering their point of view, their ideas, and their view of the situation and how it should be. They are also positive, expect to succeed, assume that others will respond to their needs and interest, and take the attitude that they never lose but only sometimes need a little more time to win.

B: LAMBS Lambs are loyal and gentle. A lamb is the type who says she will do anything for you and really means it. A lamb's loyalty causes her to go the last mile for anyone to whom the lamb is loyal. They are also recognizable by their gentleness, ability to go with the flow, and the certain knowledge that they will never become aggressive, abrasive, or menacing.

3-A: BEARS Bears are spontaneous and relaxed. Their spontaneity results in their being a lot of fun, easy to be around much of the time, and always ready to be part of the action and usually responsible for spontaneously initiating the action. Bears also appear to be quite relaxed, laid back, and always in control. They do have a tendency to go into hibernation if things get a little out of their control or are not quite the way they want them to be and also have a tendency to get a little carried away with what are sometimes bone-crushing bear hugs when they want to press their point, with those "hugs" coming up fairly spontaneously and a little unpredictably.

B: BEAVERS Beavers are very responsible and open. They do what is expected, always follow through with their commitments, and are intent on taking care of the piece of the world that has been assigned to them. This responsibility combines with openness to make them very accepting, very up front and sharing, and willing to work with anyone under almost any circumstances. Their sense of responsibility does get a little rigid sometimes in terms of doing things the way they are supposed to be done whether that is exactly what the situation calls for or not. Their openness may occasionally be seen as gullibility and does have the tendency to make them vulnerable to those who are less scrupulous. Nonetheless, they do what they do very well, especially if it is not of concern that they seem to have virtually no capacity to do other than what they do.

4-A: TIGERS Tigers are energetic and attractive. They are real go-getters who enjoy taking on a challenge to which they can bring nearly boundless energy. They are also extremely attractive in terms of others being attracted to them. Their attractiveness draws a crowd to them quickly; and they have the good fortune of having the energy to deal with all of the attention. They are great at getting things started but sometimes may lack a little in the follow through or persistence department. It has also been pointed out that tigers are sexy which is not surprising since they are obviously attractive and do have the energy to "stay out all night and cat around:" a good pasttime for a tiger.

B: TURTLES Turtles are dependable and patient. They can be counted on in the short run and in the long run. This includes sticking to the path, persevering under difficult circumstances, and an ability to endure the gusty winds and bumpy roads inherent in the journey. Their patience really is a virtue of the first order, giving them the ability to wait until it all blows over or things clear up. They do have a tendency to crawl into their shells when the going gets tough or stress gets high; but they are well protected within the shell and will always be there when the time comes to start again. They have also been seen as extremely thorough and able to do a job, especially if it doesn't matter how long it takes.

5-A: BUZZARDS Buzzards are flexible and supportive. They have the long view, the broad perspective, and are very good about cleaning up the messes of others. They are what has been described as troubleshooters and problem finders, although their problem solving is sometimes excessive and may seem like overkill. They are also supportive, since they do not need a goal and mission of their own. They can get involved sometimes without even being asked and will support which ever cause or side they happen to be on at the time. Nonetheless, it is important to emphasize the buzzard's ability to adjust to almost any difficult or complex situation, his ability to find problems where there may not have been any that were obvious to any one else, and his willingness to work toward whatever end seems most appropriate and expedient at the time.

B: BEES Bees are consistent and accepting. Their consistency allows them to do the things they do in a regular and predictable way. They are easy to be around since their styles are so recognizable and definable. They are also accepting and seem not to mind changes in situations or circumstances, the ups and downs experienced by others with whom they associate, and the fact that the world is not always as others think it should always be. These positive qualities are only somewhat diminished by the bee's tendency to "stick it to you" when you might least expect it because the bee is so sweet and honey like that it is hard to get upset or annoyed with her, although things do get a little sticky from time to time.

(Note) It really is a jungle out there and is also important to understand the animals and to understand the animal group to which you belong. There is also the socialized civilized side of things, though. This is where consideration and tolerance come in. They are not of the nature of individuals but need to be learned over time and carefully cultivated. Using a 5-point scale with 5 representing very high, 4 representing high, 3 representing medium, 2 representing low, and 1 representing very low, how would you rate your self in terms of being considerate with others in your family? Using the same rating scale, how would you rate yourself in terms of being tolerant with other people in your family? Can you give three examples of your being considerate and three of your being tolerant to support your rating?

DISCUSSION

If this activity is compared to the interpersonal style type activity, it will be seen that the sharks, lions, bears, tigers, and buzzards reflect the same elements or characteristics as were attributed to dictators and levitators. Further, seals, lambs, beavers, turtles, and bees reflect the same elements or characteristics as were attributed to facilitators and gravitators. This activity may, then, be understood in relationship to and as an extension of the earlier, interpersonal style type activity.

Ordinarily, individuals participating in the activity will tend to identify both with group A: sharks-lions-bears-tigers-buzzards and with group B: seals-lambs-beavers-turtles-bees. The fact is that their day-to-day functioning may actually reflect this mixed and blended pattern. The tendency is, though, for them to move nearly exclusively toward the A group or the B group during times of stress, tension, conflict, confusion, or ambiguity. The tendency is to move into their comfort zones.

Group A individuals tend, by nature, to be more aggressive and individualistic, while members of group B tend to be more passive and socially-oriented. Although individuals sometimes have difficulty recognizing this comfort zone tendency, others members of the family usually have no difficulty assigning each family member to one of the two groups.

Once the consultant has facilitated the client's identifying the group in which she best fits, education begins to focus on the effect of socialization on this natural style and on the client's ability to recognize and modify the style during times of stress, confusion, or interpersonal ambiguity. The activity becomes a measure of the extent to which the client is experiencing stress insofar as she will tend to go to the extremes within group A or the extremes within group B, moving in a direction consistent with her natural tendency. Understanding and recognizing this tendency is, then, the first step in developing more socialized, more effective style during times of stress.

Group A individuals learn to recognize their typical stress reactions in terms of the characteristics designating their group. They will find themselves becoming more intensely focused on and preoccupied with the situations and individuals with whom they are interacting. Their involvement becomes very intense and tends to exclude other interests and activities. At times, this may take on an almost obsessive quality. They also develop an increased need to be decisive, make something happen, and take charge of both the situation and of other people in the situation.

This group A tendency compounds in terms of being more forceful and assertive sometimes edging on aggressiveness. The individual's level of spontaneity shifts to what is easily perceived by others as insensitivity and a lack of concern for their feelings and thoughts. The intense control experienced by the individual is intended to convey an attitude of relaxed positiveness and confidence. The underlying tension and anxiety, however, come through and are easily seen by others as the primary state of the individual. Group A people under extreme stress take on a driven quality with their normally energetic and attractive approach becoming overwhelming and, to some extent, overbearing. The usual responses they get from others to their flexibility and supportiveness are quickly replaced by a reciprocal anxiety and quality of apprehension. The group A person has become, from the point of view of others, unpredictable and potentially dangerous in socioemotional terms. Along with experiencing extreme stress, she becomes a stress carrier, quickly transferring her stress and tension to others.

Group B individuals in times of extreme stress begin to manifest that stress through similar tendencies toward the opposite extremes. Their natural helpfulness becomes a need to do things for others and to be all things to all people. Their nervousness and apprehension are managed through seeming to take little seriously and seeming as if they think everyone wants to play and not really deal with the serious issues or concerns. In this sense, their attitude is sometimes perceived by others as somewhat childish and inappropriate.

Type B individuals also begin to find their security in being loyal to others without rational appraisal of the goals and directions inherent in this unquestioning loyality. Their normal gentleness becomes passivity and increases their vulnerability. This is compounded by their openness that becomes excessive in the direction of self-disclosure and an absence of self-protection. Their sense of responsibility intensifies and increases to the point of becoming a self-imposed burden which compounds with an increased need to be seen as dependable which may result in their pushing themselves past the point of responsible participation. What is usually a very desirable quality of patience becomes an inability to act, developing a quality of socioemotional immobilization.

The result of these tendencies is a high level of ambiguity and uncertainty that results in increased anxiety and tension as a result of a perceived inability to consistently play their parts in the group. At this point, their usually appealing, accepting approach to others moves into the realm of fatalism and powerlessness and a sense of being defeated and unappreciated.

Whether extreme stress moves one toward the group A adaptation of the sharks or the group B adaptation of the seals, the effect is counterproductive for the individual. This is true whether the tendency is mild or more toward the extreme. In either event, the individual needs to move more toward a socialized, interpersonal adaptation. With the support and coaching of the consultant, both the sharks and the seals learn to develop early awareness of and recognition of stress reactions and adaptational patterns in themselves. Once this recognition has occurred and has been accompanied by education directed to understanding the reaction pattern, consultation focuses in terms of more effective self-management and interpersonal participation.

Sharks will find that their stress levels reduce as they become more helpful and playful, loyalty-oriented and gentle, sensitive to their interpersonal responsibilities and more open with others, conscious of being there for others and being a dependable participant, developing a longer perspective with increased patience and more socioemotional consistency, and simply being more accepting of others, who they are, and what their needs and interests are. Sharks best manage stress reactions by emulating the strengths of the seals, with the seals achieving the same end through emulating the strengths of the sharks.

ACTIVITY 9

INTERPERSONAL PRIORITY SETTING

AS YOU RELATE to people in your family, you will find that things go better if emphasis is given to cooperation, loyalty, caring, sharing, respect, and trust. First, simply think about your family relationships. Do people cooperate with you? Are people loyal to you? Do your family members care about you and share with you? Do you think you receive the level of respect and trust you would like to have? The idea in this activity is for you to evaluate yourself in terms of being someone who gets cooperation, loyalty, caring, sharing, respect, and trust from others.

Using the scale from five to one, rate yourself on each of the six statements below. Five equals almost always, four equals usually, three equals sometimes, two equals seldom, and one equals almost never. Once you are finished, add your ratings together and divide the total by six. This will give you a priority score. It will be in your best interest to relate to others in your family in ways that keep your priority score at 4.0 or higher. When you are having difficulties with family relationships, go back to this activity, think about the statements, and then devote some time for two or three weeks to being sure that your priority score stays above 4.0.

___1. COOPERATION I am consistently helpful to others in my family.

___2. LOYALTY I hang in there in a positive way with the ups and downs in the relationships with people in my family.

___3. CARING I am consistently involved and interested in others in my family.

___4. SHARING I spend some time talking with members of my family everyday.

___5. RESPECT I listen patiently and carefully whenever members of my family are talking, telling me about something, or trying to express their ideas or feelings.

___6. TRUST I do not get into blaming, accusing, or threatening members of my family.

DISCUSSION

This activity is designed to focus on and emphasize the importance of the relationship to the client and to articulate those qualities or characteristics within the relationship that are valued: those that result in the most satisfaction and sense of fulfillment within the relationship. The activity also emphasizes the reciprocal nature of these priorities and translates those priorities into behavioral, "doable" activities and approaches. To the extent that the client manifests these behaviors and approaches within her relationships, she will experience an increased sense of cooperation, loyalty, caring, sharing, respect, and trust within the feedback loop from others. It is a fairly simply strategy, e.g., if you are more helpful to others they are more likely to be helpful to you, if you hang in there with them they are more likely to hang in there with you.

In more specific terms, the client wants to increase the level of cooperation she experiences in relationships with other family members. This will best be achieved by looking for and taking advantage of opportunities to be helpful to others in big and small ways. Importantly, though, this helpfulness must be something that is consistent and predictable to develop the optimal cooperative level of feedback from others.

The same principle applies to increasing the extent to which the client perceives other family members as being loyal to her. Importantly, loyalty is most clearly perceived in a direct and personal way and develops in terms of the relationship. The attitude and approach comes in terms of, "We have our ups and downs, good days and bad days, times when we are feeling good about each other and times when we are not. Sometimes we handle these fluctuations better and sometimes less effectively; but our relationship endures." It is also important that this commitment to each other through the relationship maintains a positive willing quality: a quality of conscious, voluntary participation in the relationship. The relationship never becomes a "have to" type of thing. There is not room for either the saint or the martyr in the reality of a healthy family.

An illustration may be useful. A young boy came to his father, suitcase in hand, saying, "I am going to run away from home." Somewhat surprised and a little puzzled, the father said, "No, you are not going to run away from home. I do not run away from home, your mother does not run away from home, and you are not going to run away from home. Running away is not the way we deal with each other or with our problems. We hang in there—good days, bad days, and all." The five year old was somewhat taken aback but said, "Oh, I thought it would be okay." The father then said, "Being upset is okay, and sometimes being really mad is also okay. Let's talk about what's going on."

Being cared about is a high priority for the client. She best assures this by understanding that a sense of caring comes through seeing that others are voluntarily involved with and interested in her. Again, the process is reciprocal. The client needs to focus more time and energy in terms of being more actively involved with others in her family and demonstrating an increased interest in them and their activities. Importantly, this increasing involvement and interest needs to be pursued on a very consistent basis and should not fluctuate based on the immediate mood or interest of the client. She must consistently increase caring behavior if she is to increase the extent to which she feels cared about.

Sharing is, thus, very closely linked with caring and as the concept is developed here is primarily pursued in verbal, talking terms. The client needs to talk more with others on a consistent, daily basis if they are to spend more time talking with her. Talking with each other becomes, then, the sharing dimension within the caring family.

Respect and trust function in tandem, much like caring and sharing. They are also similarly reciprocal. Listening to others is at least as important as talking with and actively interacting with them. Simply taking in what is said is not enough, however. The client first needs to listen patiently, which involves being relaxed, actively trying to understand what the other person is saying instead of thinking about what she is going to say, and being sure that the other person has finished before responding. A useful technique is to clarify what the other person has said before responding to it. For example, "I understand you to be saying. . . . If I correctly understand, . . . (now comes the response)." This assures that the client is carefully listening as well as patiently listening. She will find, over time, that through these techniques others gradually come to listen to her in more patient and caring ways.

It is additionally important that the response or reaction to either what the other person is saying or to her behavior reflects a quality of acceptance of the other person and does not involve blaming, accusing, or threatening. The goal is for the client to develop more effective communication. Arguing and negatively relating to the other person is never an appropriate approach to meaningful and effective communication. This in no way precludes disagreements, differing opinions and interpretations, or opposing points of view. It simply reflects an effective approach for communicating about whatever is going on, whatever the issues are.

The goal is to maximize cooperation, loyalty, caring, sharing, respect, and trust. Negativism, arguing, blaming, threatening, and accusing only serve to reduce the presents of priorities within the relationships.

ACTIVITY 10

UNDERLYING INTERPERSONAL PROCESSES

IT WILL BE most helpful if you complete activity 9 (Interpersonal Priority Setting) before working on this activity. When you are ready, the idea here is to look at how well you manage your relationships within your family. The better you become at relationship management, the more satisfying and useful the relationships in your family will be for you. Rate yourself on each of the seven statements below using a scale from five to one. Five equals almost always, four equals usually, three equals sometimes, two equals seldom, and one equals almost never.

When you experience difficulties in your relationships within your family, come back to these seven statements and consider how you are doing. It will be helpful to add your seven ratings together for the seven statements and then divide the total by seven. You are on the right track when you maintain a process score of 4.0 or higher.

The seven capitalized words at the beginning of the statements simply give names to the seven processes. DIRECTION is a process that helps direct or move relationships in ways that are useful to you. ACTION encourages others to respond to and support your needs and interests. ATTITUDE MANAGEMENT encourages others to see you in a positive light. DISTANCING encourages others to stay close enough to you and available enough to you to be there for you at all times. MAINTAINING ENGAGEMENT is a very closely related idea that helps meet your need to always feel that you belong and are part of the family. MANAGING CONFLICT helps assure that your family relationships are as comfortable for you as they can be. MODELING is a process that you involve yourself in to better assure that others in your family will behave and relate to you in ways that are pleasing and satisfying to you.

___1. DIRECTION I keep the commitments I make to and agreements I make with members of my family.
___2. ACTION I think about, understand, and support the needs and interests of members of my family.
___3. ATTITUDE MANAGEMENT I maintain a flexible approach with members of my family, relating to each member in ways that are most useful to and comfortable for him/her.
___4. DISTANCING I am sure that the members of my family get acknowledgment, time, and attention from me on a regular basis.
___5. MAINTAINING ENGAGEMENT I consistently show my interest in the activities and problems of others in my family.
___6. MANAGING CONFLICT I identify, define, and work on resolving any points of conflict or tension that come up in my relationships with people in my family.
___7. MODELING Within my family, I behave and relate to others as I would like for them to behave and to relate to me.

DISCUSSION

This section modifies the approach from earlier "discussion" sections somewhat. Here, attention is on both the above activity and the preceeding activity dealing with interpersonal priorities. It is, thus, important to complete activity 9 prior to proceeding with this section.

The interpersonal processes in this activity may be thought of as supporting and furthering the priorities in activity 9. As a preliminary step, it will be helpful to extend the behavioral manifestations of the priorities in the earlier activity. This is accomplished by simply extending the behavioral directives associated with the priorities. Once this is done, the same extention approach may be applied to the interpersonal processes. The result is a more extensive set of priority statements combined with a similarly extended set of process statements. When necessary for purposes of clarity, these extentions are accompanied by brief exclamations and elaborations.

PRIORITIES: Initiating reciprocal cooperation begins with the client's being clear with himself and other family members about what is wanted and expected. Developing clarity with reference to expectations requires careful work on the part of the consultant in assisting the client to first see himself as having expectations and then in assisting the client to define and articulate those expectations in terms that enable other family members to respond. The client needs to be additionally assisted in helping other members of the family to define and articulate their expectations. Within this environment of clear expectations, then, all members of the family can better pitch in and work with each other both in terms of shared expectations and in terms of those expectations that are unique to specific members of the family.

Next, the client and the consultant will want to focus on loyalty as a reciprocal and shared aspect of family life. At a very fundamental level, this depends on the client's valuing being part of the family. "Do you value being part of your family? Is being part of your family important to you?" Most clients will somewhat automatically and reflexively respond to these questions in the affirmative. At that point, the consultant may help by facilitating the definition of "valuing."

"I hear you saying that you value being part of your family. A lot of people feel that way and were we to ask other members of your family, they would probably say the same thing. I have found that it is important that these types of feelings are given more than superficial lip service. What do you value about being a part of your family?" The consultant and client may then work on developing a prioritized list of four or five factors that the client values. That which is valued then becomes the driver or that which most nearly guarantees continuing loyalty.

It also becomes the underlying reason for developing faith in other members of the family as the client has experience with them as people who provide and assure those things valued by the client. Experience with family members as providers of those things valued by the client generalizes to valuing the members themselves and having faith in them in more comprehensive and meaningful terms.

Caring for each other at a reciprocal level within the family is encouraged and furthered by having pride in each other. This starts with the client's having a sense of pride in each member of his family. "Are you proud of the other members of your family? If so, what are sources of pride for you? Let's think about each member of your family and see if we can develop a list of two or three things about each person that results in your being proud of him. We are not particularly looking for things that you like or appreciate about other family members. Here, we are looking for things that make you feel good about you just because you are in the same family with the other person." In addition to focus on the idea of pride, this exercise also encourages and enables the client to begin to understand that his sense of self and self-esteem depend, in part, on who the other members of his family are. Part of his pride in who he is depends on who they are. At this level of insight, then, the client may easily see that it is in his interest and in the interest of his self-esteem to support and encourage other members of the family, to support and encourage their activities, interest, and involvements.

Supporting and encouraging each other within the family extends to sharing with each other in caring and meaningful ways. Along with talking with each other, this sharing needs to include an atmosphere of openness and up-frontness with each other.

Failing to share with each other in direct and clear ways what one thinks, feels, and believes about each member of the family jeopardizes the caring environment and directly interferes with cooperation and any continuing sense of loyalty. The client may say, "I think this is a good idea but being open and up-front is not something I do very well. I know what I think and feel but am not very good at expressing it." The consultant may then help the client understand that the goal is not perfection, showing that he was already interpersonally skilled, or being able to do things that one can not yet do. The goal within the family is for the client to give it his best shot, to try being more open and up-front, to gradually increase his ability to contribute positively to a sharing environment.

This level of sharing is best achieved within an environment characterized by mutual respect. As suggested in activity 9, respect begins with listening to each other patiently and carefully. By reflecting this level of respect with other family members, the client not only conveys respect but begins to learn about sharing. He will see how others express themselves, are open with the client, and try to deal with him in up-front and candid ways. He will also find that, having been given the opportunity to express themselves, other members of the family are significantly more receptive to the client's efforts to express himself.

Among other things, the client's respect for other members of the family conveys to them a willingness on the part of the client to accept them as they are. Following the principle of reciprocity, this orientation on the part of the client increases the willingness of other family members to accept him on an as-is basis. The atmosphere of mutual acceptance, then, makes sharing and cooperation easier and smoother.

The above leads to a quality of trust within family relationships enabling each family member to be more comfortable and at ease with other family members. At a fundamental level, trust is the key to assuring the other five priorities: cooperation, loyalty, caring, sharing, and respect. The effect is a give and take relationship among and between family members, with an absence of significant criticism, jeopardy, or potential rejection.

It is a sense of or fear of rejection that is perhaps the single greatest factor interfering with comfortable, satisfying, and effective intrafamily relationships. Consciously increasing trust within the family, then, directly reduces one of the major negative drivers within the family: a fear of rejection or nonacceptance. The client moves into a position where he may depend on other members of the family and count on them to be there and to do what needs to be done. They may not always be happy with the client, feel good about him, or relate to him in positive ways. Nonetheless, the underlying trust within the family assures everyone that they will all deal with the ups and downs, good times and bad times.

PROCESSES: Direction helps move relationships in ways that are useful to the client. As suggested earlier, this process starts with keeping commitments and agreements with other family members. In addition, the process is furthered by an approach geared toward influencing other family members instead of directing or trying to control them and or their activities. The client should learn to make suggestions instead of giving directives, ask instead of telling, explain instead of demanding.

It is important for him to understand that, over time, it really is true—as the old saying suggests—"You accomplish more with honey than with vinegar." People will usually move in the direction you want them to move if they are asked, if they understand why it is important, and if they know that their doing so is appreciated.

This appreciation is expressed in general and direct ways. At the same time, though, it is important to focus any criticism in very direct and specific ways. Praise and express appreciation in lavish and general terms. Express any criticism or negative feelings in very limited and specific ways. Through the process, the client will gradually get to a point where he is more clearly directing relationships in ways useful to him, responding to those problem points or negative times in very limited and specific ways, and clearly letting others know that their helpful approach is appreciated.

The action process within family relationships encourages others to respond to the client in ways that support and compliment his needs and interest. Following the principle of reciprocity, the action process is furthered by the client's understanding and supporting the needs and interest of other members of the family. "What do other members of the family need? What is important to them? What can you do to support these needs and interests?" On a reciprocal basis, the client is clear about what he needs, his interest, what he expects.

The client needs to be consistent with reference to his needs and interest and the articulation of those needs and interest to others. Additionally, he needs to be firm about his needs and interest and the expectation that other family members take them into consideration. This firmness must not turn into aggression, a demanding approach, or an approach that indicates that the client's needs and interests are more important than those of others. Here, gentle firmness is the key.

The process of attitude management encourages others to see the client in a positive light. Attention to the first two processes—direction and action—facilitates this positive perception of the client.

In addition, seeing each member of the family as an individual and individualizing one's approach, relationship, and expectations furthers the attitude management process. "How is your approach to each member of your family different from your approach to each other member of the family? How does this result in differences in your relationships with each member? What are the differences? What do you expect from each member of your family; and how are those expectations different from those held for other members of the family?" Implicit in this individualization is a level of flexibility that will allow the client to respond differentially to the special needs and interest of each family member. This, in turn, enables the client to emphasize and facilitate the satisfaction of each member of the family. On a reciprocal basis, this, in turn, increases the likelihood of their encouraging and facilitating the general level of satisfaction of the client. "If I help you be more satisfied with who you are and with being a part of the family, the likelihood is that your functioning in relationship to me will have a similar effect for me."

The distancing process combines with the other interpersonal processes to encourage other members of the family to stay close and in touch with the client and available to him. In order to further this process, the client must assure that each member of the family receives acknowledgement and recognition from him on a regular basis. Importantly, though, it is not enough to simply say "hello." Acknowledgement and recognition come through knowing of the other person's interest and activities, keeping up with their involvements and interest, and taking time to know who they are on a day-to-day basis. Collectively, these represent who the other person is. It is to whom the person is that one gives acknowledgment and recognition.

The idea is to convey a real and felt sense that says, "I know who you are, am interested in you and who you are, and enjoy being close enough with you to keep in touch and up to date." On a reciprocal basis, of course, other members of the family are more likely to relate to the client on the same basis. Important here is a willingness to simply accept fluctuations in the attitudes, behaviors, and involvements of other family members. Sometimes people feel closer to each other and sometimes they feel a little more distant. Nonetheless, the client works toward maintaining the distance at a close and relating level as much of the time as possible.

Among other things, this means that the client is as willing to adjust to and adapt to other family members as he expects them to be willing to adjust to or adapt to him. This principle of each adapting to the other in flexible and mutually accommodating ways is especially important within parent/child relationships and within the marriage dyad. The client should simply keep in mind that accommodating and adjusting to others is not an unlimited process. It should not develop into a game as discussed in an earlier activity. It is, instead, a process related to distancing within relationships and to maintaining a close, in touch involvement with each other.

The process is probably best understood in relationship to maintaining engagement leading to always feeling that one belongs and is part of the family. This starts with assuring that the client interacts with other members of the family on a regular basis and that they interact with him. In addition, though, maintaining engagement suggest that the client should take additional responsibility to be sure that there is time and opportunity for other members of the family to interact with each other. Importantly, the environment within which these interactions take place should be maintained in a positive, comfortable manner, to the extent that the client is able to influence these environmental qualities. Within this process, conveying interest needs to be managed in a direct way. It is not enough to talk with others about a family member, to tell others about his accomplishments or achievements, or to discuss with them problems or difficulties one may be having with another family member. These things should be managed directly with each member of the family following the processes of direction, action, attitude management, and so on.

The client may encourage each family member to be experimental, to suggest new ideas and approaches to be used to better manage engagement with each other. At the family level, it might be well to simply sit down with each other and talk about this process, listening carefully to the ideas and suggestions of each member. The client may be surprised to find how much assistance he will receive from other family members if they are simply invited to participate in thinking about the process.

Conflict management is a critical process within any family and represents one of the most important skill areas in the development of effective interpersonal relationships. When handled well, conflict management assures that members of the family are as comfortable with the client as they can be. As suggested earlier, a fear of nonacceptance or rejection is one of the primary negative drivers within families. Conflict fuels that driver perhaps more than any other single factor. Managing conflict, then, leads to minimizing any sense of rejection or nonacceptance on the part of family members.

Effective conflict management starts with the client's simply tolerating a fairly high level of ambiguity or uncertainty in the behavior of other family members and in his relationships with them. It relates back to having faith in them and to accepting them on an as is basis. Much family conflict revolves around misunderstandings, differing opinions, pressing for explanations where no explanation is readily available, and pushing other individuals to remove any ambiguity or lack of clarity that may be present. In addition, there are going to be those points of tension, conflict, increased negativism. Most individuals are somewhat naturally tempted to try to deal with these points and resolve them. Much of the time, it is in the interest of conflict management to simply absorb or tolerate these periods of high dissonance or conflict and those occasional periods of mild dissonance or conflict. The idea is to use an approach that absorbs the intense negative feelings and tries to understand what is happening, how people are feeling, and what is driving the tension or conflict. It is at this level that a response is appropriate, although many times one might be better off to simply understand that people are in a bad mood sometimes, feel tense sometimes, and behave in ways that cause conflict and negative feelings.

So long as the problems are not chronic or persistent, these occasional episodes of dissonance or conflict are simply part of being in the family and probably do not need any specific response. The family system really does crunch and bump sometimes. The key is to be alert to real problems, things that really do need resolution and continuing attention. This is especially true if the same difficulties keep coming up over and over again or if a specific family member seems to be the brunt of or the source of the conflict on a regular or recurring basis. In these situations, attention is less to the conflict itself and more toward that which is causing or contributing to the conflict.

Modeling is perhaps the most significant of the seven interpersonal processes being discussed here. Through the educational approach, the client not only learns to function in more interpersonally effective ways with style but also begins to represent a model or example within the family of interpersonally effective style. He begins to exemplify family priorities and becomes an individual whom others emulate. Part of this modeling process involves emphasizing positive things, ideas, interpretations, and processes within the family, giving direct and very clear attention to any problems or difficulties that may arise. "I understand that you are feeling fairly negative about your family relationships and about other people in the family. Others in your situation have felt much the same way. I have found, though, that your continuing to verbalize and express these negative things and ideas only tends to make the family environment more negative. I think you may find that working on the problems, working on how you relate to others, working on the example you set for others may, in the long run, do a lot more good than simply talking about how bad things are without taking personal responsibility for your style, your involvement, your participation, your role in what is going on. You may not be able to do much at this point about what is going on with others. You can and should, however, do what you can do to be a person with style, all the time, on purpose."

ACTIVITY 11

BE NICE TO YOURSELF

THIS ACTIVITY may be approached in several ways, depending on the special needs of the group and the particular situation in which the activity is used. It may be used as an outline or guide for a creative presentation to groups of young children, may be used as a discussion guide with groups especially when the groups include both adults and children, and may be used as an interview format when working with individual children and families. The goal of the activity is to encourage a nurturing attitude toward self, an awareness of factors related to positive mental health, and an orientation to talking and sharing with others as a way of eliciting guidance and affirmation.

POSITIVE MENTAL HEALTH

1. What do you think it means to have good mental health?
2. What do you do to help your mental health?
3. What do you like about yourself?
4. What helps you feel happy, excited, satisfied? What kinds of people, situations, things help you feel good, help you be emotionally positive?
5. When do you feel unhappy? What kinds of people, situations, or things get you to feeling afraid, angry, sad, confused, or feeling emotionally negative?
6. Sometimes our negative emotions get out of balance and sort of take over. When this happens, we sometimes have problems with our behavior and adjustment. When your emotions get a little out of balance and the negative emotions take over, what kinds of problems does it cause you with your behavior, your adjustment?

HAVING GOOD MENTAL HEALTH

7. Our feelings are okay. This includes feeling afraid, angry, or sad. How we deal with our feelings makes a difference, though. How do you deal with it when you feel angry, when you feel afraid, when you feel sad?
8. It is important to understand our anger and to express it appropriately. How do you express your anger? How do you let people know when you are angry?
9. It is important to understand our fears and to talk about them. What do you think is going on with you when you feel afraid? With whom do you talk about your fears?
10. Being said is normal. Understanding why we are sad and sharing our sadness with someone else is an important part of good mental health. With whom do you share your sadness?
11. When our negative emotions get out of balance, it is important to try to understand and share those emotions with others. It is also important to get our emotions back into balance. When you are experiencing negative emotions, what kinds of things do you do to get things back into balance, to help yourself feel more emotionally positive?

PEOPLE WANT TO HELP

12. The first person who can help you is you. You do this by being nice to yourself. What do you do to be sure that these nice things happen for you?—Sharing your feelings with others—Being positively involved with other people—Being cheerful with other people—Being helpful to other people—Enjoying a well balanced diet—Getting plenty of sleep—Trying new things—Keeping a good balance of work, rest, and play—Getting held when you need it—Giving and getting hugs—Not abusing or misusing alcohol or drugs—Being as nice to others as you would like them to be to you.
13. Feel good about yourself and others will feel good about you. Be nice to yourself—you deserve it. What have you done today to be nice to yourself? What will you do tomorrow to be nice to yourself? You are a special person. You are a person with style, all the time, on purpose.

PART THREE

THE EDUCATIONAL APPROACH WITHIN PARENT/CHILD RELATIONSHIPS

INTRODUCTION

THE CONSULTATION APPROACH

THE ACTIVITIES in this section are designed to assist in the rapid assessment of children and adolescents, rapid assessment of the parent/child relationship, and development of an early intervention parenting plan. It is also important to emphasize those situations where these activities are not likely to be useful and may be inappropriate. Specifically, other more comprehensive methodologies are needed for children and adolescents who have an extended history of serious maladjustment, who are known to have serious psychiatric or psychological problems, or who reflect severe episodes of behavioral disturbance. The activities here are for the majority of young people who are experiencing minor to moderate interpersonal and adjustment difficulties. Similarly, the activities are not particularly useful when working with families known to be seriously dysfunctional, having a history of family violence, showing serious instability over an extended period of time, or including a seriously disturbed or dysfunctional adult. The activities are for the majority of families who are experiencing mild to moderate adjustment and interpersonal difficulties.

With the assistance of the consultant, parents and children can work together to develop a parenting plan responsive to the results of the child assessment and responding to the strengths and problem areas raised in the parent assessment activities.

When developing the parenting plan and participating in the consultation process, it is important to maintain focus on a "how to" basis, using the feel-felt-found technique developed earlier. In addition, what is understood as the RECIPES approach is also useful. Here, RECOGNITION of problems and difficulties leads to involvement with the consultant in EDUCATION related to the problems and difficulties. This CONSULTATION enables the family to better understand the problems and difficulties, strengths and assets that have developed over time. INTERVENTION then comes through continuing work with the family to better understand the issues and strengths and develop techniques and approaches that best respond to them within the context of the unique family. PRACTICE then becomes key to successfully emphasizing the strengths and assets within the family and minimizing the problems and difficulties. EXPERIENCE with the new insights and techniques will have the positive effective of improved family functioning which will, in turn, reinforce continuation of the educational process. SUPPORT on the part of the consultant through coaching and encouragement and coming from family members who respond positively to the new relationships and involvements concludes the self-reinforcing quality of the educational approach and the general enhancement of the functioning of the family system.

Keep in mind that the approach is educational and supportive. In this sense, it is important to avoid the temptation to drift into psychotherapy and/or family system reconstruction.

The last activity in this section focuses on developmental parenting. It assists parents in achieving a multidimensional understanding of parenting and facilitates developing a congruence between the developmental age and stage of the youngster and the approach and style of parenting. This activity gives renewed emphasis to the point that parenting follows from and is an integral part of positive interpersonal relationships and must take into consideration the child, the parent, who each is as an individual, and what is most useful to the child and supportive of his/her ongoing growth and development.

ACTIVITY 12

RAPID ASSESSMENT OF YOUNGSTERS

THIS ACTIVITY is useful when assessing the behavior, adjustment, and functioning of a young person. Importantly, it does not represent a thorough diagnostic evaluation and should not be seen as a substitute for careful, professional assessment when a specific youngster is experiencing serious or ongoing difficulties. It is, rather, only intended to point out those areas in which a child or adolescent is getting along fairly well and those areas where he/she may be having some mild, temporary difficulties.

Use a rating scale from five to one for each item on the list below. Five equals almost always, four equals usually, three equals sometimes, two equals seldom, and one equals almost never.

Note that the rating process for this activity is not the same as for the earlier activities. In this activity, each item needs to be evaluated and understood by itself. A normal, healthy young person would receive all fours and fives. Concern needs to be raised in any area suggested by an item where the young person's rating is three or below. Ratings of two or below or several ratings of three or below begin to suggest the need for more extensive assessment and more traditional therapeutic involvements.

THE YOUNG PERSON

___ 1. Is energentic and interested in what is going on around him/her.
___ 2. Feels attractive.
___ 3. Is relaxed and comfortable with himself/herself.
___ 4. Likes himself/herself.
___ 5. Is self-confident.
___ 6. Has a normal appetite and eating habits.
___ 7. Stays away from drugs and alcohol.

___ 8. Is happy and in a positive mood.
___ 9. Manages his/her temper and anger responsibly.
___10. Is honest and truthful.
___11. Is a good student.
___12. Feels successful.
___13. Likes school.
___14. Finishes projects, assignments, or other things for which he/she is responsible.
___15. Is well behaved.
___16. Is easy for parents, teachers, and other adults to deal with.
___17. Is a responsible person.
___18. Is a dependable person.
___19. Has friends his/her age.
___20. Makes good choices when it comes to friends.
___21. Gets along well with his/her friends.
___22. Follows the rules and goes along with what is expected of him/her at school and at home.
___23. Makes friends easily.
___24. Is adventurous and willing to try new things.
___25. Handles day to day stresses and tensions well.
___26. Is healthy.
___27. Will talk about things with parents or other adults.

DISCUSSION

Understanding parent/child relationships and developing a parenting approach requires first that an assessment is done with and for the young person. Parenting is not a formula activity or something one does to a child. It is, rather, something one does with a child based on an understanding of and awareness of who that child is, his special problems and difficulties, and the child's unique personality. Further, good parenting depends on the style and personality of the parent, with the individuality of the parent combining with that of the child to develop an effective, on-going, on-growing relationship within which both the parent and the child may function successfully and effectively.

It is also important to understand that parenting is not an adequate response to many children and to their problems and difficulties. Parenting has the capacity to nurture and support the growth and development of relatively healthy, relatively normal children. When children begin developing problems and difficulties, however, parenting is frequently not an adequate response; and for children with special needs, parenting is simply not enough. For these children, a "parenting plus" plan needs to be developed, with that plan providing healthy, positive parenting for the child and additionally providing those services and resources necessary to adequately respond to the special needs of the youngster.

In this activity, focus is on reasonably normal, reasonably healthy children. For them, effective parenting is usually an adequate response to their growth and development, an adequate response to the normal fluctuations in their behavior and adjustment. The activity includes a sample of factors associated with a child's being reasonably normal and healthy. If difficulties show up in the sample, however, it is critically important for the child that a more thorough medical, psychological, educational, and/or other specialized evaluation be done. In addition, it is important that a parenting plus plan be developed to respond to the special needs and difficulties of the youngster.

Normal children are energetic and interested in what is going on around them. No, they are not always energetic and not always interested. The point is that they are ordinarily people who have fairly high energy levels and who are interested in what is going on around them. They may not direct that energy to those things that parents would prefer the energy be directed to and may not be interested in those things valued by parents. Nonetheless, their youthful energy and interest are obvious as one observes them over time.

When a youngster begins to show somewhat continuing low energy and disinterest, a problem is evident. First, the child needs to be evaluated medically, with the physician's attention directed specifically to the lethargy of the youngster. If no problems are found, the next procedure — psychosocial evaluation — needs to focus on the probability that the young person is depressed. If this is found to be the case, parents will need to bring more energy to their relationship with their youngster and will need to attend more closely to his needs and interests. It is likely, however, that this normal parenting response will not be adequate. A parenting plus plan will be necessary. In this plan, parents bring more energy to the relationship and attend more closely to the needs and interest of the youngster. They carefully involve themselves in healthy, positive parenting. In addition, though, the young person may need to be involved in counseling or therapy focusing on the continuing depression. This latter activity is the "plus" in the parenting plus plan.

Normal, healthy children feel reasonably attractive in the sense that they see themselves as someone to whom others are attracted. In addition, they generally like themselves, are relatively self-confident, are ordinarily fairly happy and in a positive mood, and feel fairly successful in relation to those things valued by the youngster. Again, these feelings and perceptions are not present all the time and are not present in relation to all characteristics of the youngster or all aspects of his life. Here, attention is to the preponderance of the youngster's self-concept, his self-esteem. Also, it is important to evaluate these traits and characteristics over time, since on any particular day, a quite normal and healthy young person may feel ugly, incompetent and of little value. Even during these times, though, normal youngsters will ordinarily respond to the positive involvement and feedback of their parents.

For young people experiencing these types of difficulties, good parenting lets the child know that the parents are attracted to him. How do parents show this attraction? They spend a little more time with the youngster, focus on positives instead of negatives, sincerely acknowledge the youngster's feelings and perceptions, and let the child know that he is cared about and loved. "I enjoy spending time with you, talking with you, and having you as a member of our family. I can see that you do not like yourself very well today but want you to know that I like you and have faith in you and your abilities." Good parenting responds to the successful, competent, attractive, valued young person. If this does not facilitate his moving to a more positive space, though, additional services are needed that help both the young person and the parent better understand the issues and concerns, the problems and difficulties.

Normal children are generally relaxed and comfortable with themselves, with who they are. Being relaxed should not here suggest necessarily being calm or "laid back." The young person may be very intense, very active, and very involved in a number of things at the same time. Nonetheless, the activity and involvement do not reflect anxiety, signs of tension or stress, continuing frustration, or any significant level of discomfort or displeasure with who he is. Yes, there may be periods of tension, self-doubt, anxiety, frustration, and other negative feelings and perceptions. Nonetheless, the predominant projection is one of being reasonably relaxed and comfortable.

If the young person's pattern of adjustment and self-management begins to show anxiety, tension, and other negative or uncomfortable elements, additional evaluation and assessment are needed. At the same time, though, parents will want to emphasize being calm and relaxed with the young person, being comfortable with who he is, and convey an atmosphere of acceptance and appreciation. Parenting may also extend to working with the youngster to better understand the problems and difficulties, the sources of the tension and stress. Here, parents can exercise direct influence in terms of providing advise and guidance, managing and structuring the environment of the young person, and enabling the young person to use the adult perspective of the parent. If this is not enough, though—and at times it may not be—additional services and resources need to be incorporated into the parenting plus plan.

Healthy children reflect a normal appetite and eating habits. Generally, this is reflected through the youngster's eating when other people in the family eat, eating about the same foods other family members eat, and not reflecting any particular preoccupation with eating or eating patterns. For adolescents, however, dieting may become a mild preoccupation, although one should become concerned if the young person begins gaining or especially if the young person begins losing weight.

Does the young person look unusually heavy or unusually thin? If so, this needs evaluated by a physician on a fairly immediate basis. Also, it is important that children receive regular physical examinations, with the physician's evaluating the child's weight and eating habits as part of that examination. Here, good parenting comes first through setting a good example and encouraging good eating habits. If problems develop, however, parenting is not an adequate response to the needs of the young person. The parenting plus plan needs to include a thorough medical evaluation and may need to include specialized therapeutic services for the young person in those situations where eating disorders are suspected or confirmed. These types of difficulties are generally not managable within the family as the only resource.

This latter point also applies to the misuse or abuse of alcohol or drugs. Normal children generally stay away from the use of alcohol or drugs; and any involvement that they do have is occasional and does not reflect any continuing problem of abuse or misuse. In fact, for normal youngsters, an especially negative experience with alcohol or drugs will decrease the likelihood of the young person's having a similar negative experience in the future. The idea is that normal children learn from bad experiences, adjusting their future behavior and involvements to avoid those negative experiences. If parents suspect a problem or know that the young person has had difficulties with alcohol or drugs on more than one or two occasions, it is very important that they seek out specialized and qualified resources to incorporate into the parenting plus plan.

Normal children are reasonably honest and truthful, fairly responsible, and usually people on whom others may depend. Of course, these qualities are not at issue until the young person has reached a developmental level to begin to reflect these qualities—generally around five or six years old. Even then, it needs to be understood that honesty, dependability, and continuing responsibility are qualities that develop and become more dominant over time. Again, parenting best fosters these qualities by example. As the consultant and the client assess the example being set by parents, the consultant will want to help the client focus on small examples of honesty and truthfulness, small and large examples of responsibility, and various levels of dependability, especially as they relate to the child's being able to depend on or count on the parent. In this area, parenting is the most powerful resource available to the youngster. In fact, if these qualities are not present at a high level within the parent/child relationship, the ability of outside resources to instill these qualities in the youngster is quite limited. In this area, the educational approach is usually more effective than more traditional counseling and therapy approaches.

Normal children manage their emotions fairly well, with their ability to manage their emotions showing gradual improvement over time. By the time children are about six years old or so, they should be showing a pattern of experiencing, expressing, and managing emotions that enables them to function comfortably and smoothly within most situations. For example, the young person will experience anger and frustration and will be able to express those feelings. The expression of the anger and frustration, though, will be managed in ways that do not reflect temper tantrums, violence, destructiveness, or other negative outcomes. The emotional management will reflect an increasing pattern of positive, socialized expression that leads to healthy exercise of power, control, and influence on the part of the young person. Generally, this emotional management will reflect a primarily social, verbal pattern that is both responsible and serves the over time interest of the youngster.

The socioemotional styles of the young person's parents are as important here as they have been seen to be in other areas. Parents must be emotionally responsible and dependable if young people are expected to reflect these characteristics. In addition, though, good parenting assists the child in developing patterns of power, control, and influence that reflect positive personal style and do not have to fall back on unsocialized patterns of aggression and self-expression. If continuing problems develop, however, outside assistance is needed as part of the parenting plus plan. In addition to the child's having developed a pattern of ineffective or inappropriate emotional expression as a function of family experiences, these difficulties may also relate to medical problems, learning related difficulties, or other areas that may only be understood through competent professional evaluation and intervention. Above all, the consultant needs to focus specifically on any inclinations the parents may have to simply deal with the problems by over powering and controlling the young person.

Normal children are reasonably good students, usually like school, finish projects, assignments, or other things for which they are responsible, and deal fairly well with the school environment. This does not mean that they necessarily get all A's and B's, does not mean that they always do their homework, does not mean that they always feel good about school, and does not mean they never get into trouble at school. It means, rather, that they generally hang in there academically, passing their subjects and courses. They may not be particularly thrilled about homework or other assignments but usually make a reasonable effort to complete the requirements. They may not like particular teachers or particular classes but generally do enjoy the social interaction at school, some courses and assignments, and would generally prefer school to simply staying at home or getting a full-time job. If asked, most youngsters would indicate that they do not like school. Nonetheless, one finds that they get up and go to school voluntarily, generally enjoy themselves most of the time at school; and if they do get into trouble, those difficulties are ordinarily fairly mild and relatively inconsequential.

When children develop problems relative to these school-related areas, the most likely difficulty has to do with some type of learning problem or academically-related issue. Generally, children do as well in school as they are capable of doing at the time, all things considered. When school is not going very well for them, then, it is very important for parents to first work with the youngster in terms of trying to understand the problems and difficulties and then in terms of helping the child with the problems. If this does not get the job done, it is important that the child be evaluated by professionals who understand children, understand the school environment, and understand the very complex nature of the learning process. This evaluation will likely lead to a specialized intervention plan that becomes the "plus" in the parenting plus approach to the youngster.

The consultant will want to work with the parent in terms of the parent's attitude toward school, the attitude the parent is conveying toward the youngster, the parent's expectations, and how the parent is going about encouraging and facilitating the young person's school adjustment and academic achievement. For example, encouraging children to do their homework is a good idea. If homework becomes a battle or continuing hassle, though, the likelihood is that there are additional difficulties needing attention. It is unlikely that simply forcing the child to continue the uncomfortable, unpleasant homework activities will resolve the difficulties. In addition, this process does damage to the parent/child relationship that may have long-term negative effects. When children are having continuing difficulties in school, a parenting plus approach is essential.

Normal children are fairly well behaved, are relatively easy for parents and other adults to deal with, usually follow the rules, and usually do what is expected of them at school and at home. Children do not always behave, do not always do what is expected, do not always follow the rules, and do not always function as adults would like them to function. In fact, one would become equally concerned about a young person who never got into trouble, never broke the rules, never failed to meet expectations. The young person is adventurous, willing to and interested in trying new things, sometimes simply decides that his interest is better served by doing things his way, is sometimes overly impulsive and does not stop to think about what he is doing, and sometimes really did not understand the expectations or rules nearly as well as the adults thought he understood them. Nonetheless, the general pattern is to be reasonably conforming and cooperative.

When problems develop here, parents first need special assistance from the consultant in terms of exercising reasonable and fair discipline, being consistent, following through with appropriate and proportional negative consequences, and being clear about what is expected. This is about as far as good parenting can go. If problems persist beyond these efforts, though, outside assistance is needed in terms of evaluation of the young person, the parent/child relationship, and the special needs and interest of the youngster. It really is true that the development and personality of some children are such that normal parenting is not an adequate response to their behavior and adjustment problems. They need additional services, unusually structured environments, special assistance with learning and school related difficulties, and an unusual level of sensitivity to their special needs and adaptational patterns. In addition to assuring that the needed resources and services are available, the consultant will want to work closely with the parent to be sure that the parent is avoiding simply responding to the child's special problems by becoming increasingly frustrated and trying to simply overpower and control the youngster. Not only will these approaches be generally ineffective, they will tend over time to exacerbate or intensify the problems of the young person.

Normal children have friends their own age, make friends fairly easily, get along reasonably well with their friends, and show good choices in terms of picking friends. They are socially competent and responsible. As with areas already discussed, this area is not particularly at issue until children are about six years old or so.

This area may be the single most complex area related to the growth and development of youngsters and the parent/child relationship. First, children will tend to pick friends whom they perceive to be much like themselves. In fact, if a parent wants to know what the youngster thinks and feels about himself, one approach is to look at the friends with whom the young person associates. From the youngster's point of view, they are like him. This begins to show that the peer involvements of young people are very dependent on their levels of self-esteem, their self-concepts, their self-perceptions. This, of course, relates back to the earlier portion of this discussion related to these self-perception factors.

If a youngster is experiencing friendship related difficulties, the first level of understanding needs to be developed in terms of the parent/child relationships within which the young person is involved. Are those relationships open, accepting, warm, stable, and representative of a positive interpersonal style? Next, do the parents encourage and facilitate positive peer relationships for the youngster? Are people at home relatively spontaneous and approach-oriented in their relationships with each other? The idea is that helping young people with peer relationships starts, at a parenting level, with attention to relationships at home. Beyond that, though, peer relationships are very dependent on a young person's school adjustment, how accepted he is within the school environment, the level of physical and social skills the young person has, and the absence or presence of other physical, emotional, moral, social, sexual, or intellectual difficulties. When young people are experiencing continuing social adjustment difficulties, parenting is central to assisting with those difficulties. At the same time, though, the "plus" needs to come through additional assessments and evaluations along with additional intervention that both understands and responds to the special needs and interest of the child. Generally, this is best accomplished through counseling and ordinarily through group-level interventions emphasizing relationship development and peer interaction.

Three additional variables conclude the rapid assessment process. Normal children generally handle day-to-day stresses and tensions reasonably well. When they do not, parenting needs to focus in the areas already discussed. If this does not seem to smooth out the management process for the youngster, additional assessment and intervention—parenting plus—are required.

Normal children are reasonably healthy. This is an important but sometimes overlooked area and needs medical attention if any problems or concerns develop. The consultant will want to assist the parent in looking at minor to major health-related issues including low energy, frequent colds or infections, headaches, or other signs that the young person is not feeling well or is not functioning well physically.

Finally, normal youngsters talk about things with parents and with other adults. This includes talking about positive experiences, things that are going well, parts of their world with which they are comfortable. In addition, though, normal children seek out and talk with trusted adults when they are having difficulties, when things are not working out very well, when their lives are not going smoothly for them. Attention in this area starts within the family and emphasizes the priorities and processes discussed in earlier activities. Beyond that, though, the "plus" in the parenting plan needs to include interaction between the consultant and the youngster and the possible inclusion of counseling and ongoing guidance for the child and the family. When people are not talking with each other, the family system is shutting down. It becomes the responsibility of each member of the family and especially of the parents to assure that talking and listening are and continue to be the central aspect of family life.

ACTIVITY EXTENSION

As will have been noted, the activity as presented most appropriately applies to school-age children. The consultant will want to use the same sampling approach for the rapid assessment of younger children. In these cases, the consultant should first drop those variables from the above activity that apply less clearly to younger children. The consultant will want to simply draw on his experience, knowledge, and expertise to select those variables in the original activity that are appropriate for the specific child and are to be retained. In addition, the variables selected below may be included especially for children in the age ranges indicated. The effect is modifying the activity to correspond with the child developmentally.

Birth to Two Years Old:

1. The child responds to familiar adults and other children.
2. The child seeks out familiar adults when under stress and when she is afraid.—Seeks out with eyes, by reaching, by moving toward the adult.
3. The child becomes more comfortable with people as more time is spent with them.
4. The child has regular sleeping habits and patterns.
5. The child relates to his caretaker comfortably and easily.

Two Years to Six Years:

1. The child handles new experiences fairly well.
2. The child shows an increasing ability to use language to communicate.
3. The child shows increasing social participation.
4. The child is showing an increasing ability to delay gratification.
5. The child is reflecting increasing gross and fine motor skills and coordination.
6. The child is reflecting increasing activities and interest outside of the family.
7. The child is reflecting increasing initiative and self-control.
8. The child is reflecting increasing friendship and playmate involvements.

The following additional variables may be useful to the consultant when assessing *elementary school youngsters*.

1. The youngster is usually more interested in spending time with peers than with parents or other adults or by herself.
2. The child is able to adjust to or adapt to changes or disappointments.
3. The youngster reflects increasing frustration tolerance.
4. The youngster is able to entertain or occupy himself.
5. The youngster is content with her gender.

The following variables may be useful when assessing *adolescents*.

1. The young person reflects appropriate sexual behavior and interest.
2. The young person develops and maintains appropriate relationships with opposite sex peers.
3. The young person reflects good group level skills.
4. The judgement and decision making of the young person are consistent with his short-term and long-term self-interest.
5. The young person reflects increasingly independent judgement.
6. The young person has good driving habits.
7. The young person has a positive sense of her future.
8. The young person reflects good personal habits.

ADDENDUM

The chart in this section may be used as a convenient way of helping parents understand the nature of the problems and difficulties experienced by their children and those times when a parenting plus plan is needed. The consultant may first assist the parents in determining the primary dimension within which the problem or difficulty is present. Of course, many problems and difficulties may reflect issues in more than one dimension. Generally, though, the consultant should first encourage the parent to assign the problem or difficulty to the dimension in which it fits furthest from the bottom of the chart.

Next, the consultant may help the parent understand the type of problem being experienced by the youngster. Real problems are those that are generally understood as illnesses, diseases, conditions, or problems experienced by the young person that are unrelated to external factors or events. Real problems would be seen as problems for any child, at any time, in any situation. This may be more easily understood in comparison to relative problems. Here, the functioning of the youngster is problematic mostly in terms of how that functioning compares to the functioning of other children. Relative to other children, the youngster's functioning is somewhat delayed or problematic.

Situational problems are those problems seen in youngster whose functioning is generally free from real or relative difficulties. The particular problem comes up in relatively definable situations but is relatively absent in other situations. For example, the youngster may experience difficulties with emotional control at home but not at school, may have relationship difficulties at school but not with siblings or other children in the neighborhood, may be relatively well behaved in some situations but not in others. The problems are primarily situational.

Value based problems are perhaps the most common area of difficulty experienced between parents and children. Here, things like keeping rooms clean, good table manners, curfews, language usage, and similar value based conflicts develop. Basically, the problem is one of values and what is and is not valued. As can be seen, these types of difficulties are quite different from real problems, relative problems, and—to a lesser extent—situational problems.

When a problem or issue comes up between a parent and a child, the consultant may first assist the parent in defining the problem in very clear and specific terms. The parent may then—with the consultant's assistance—select the cell on the chart that most commonly relates to the specific problem type. Once this is done, the consultant may assist the parent in selecting other cells that "may" relate to the problem. Parenting will first respond to the first cell selected. Additional assessment and evaluation will relate to the other "possibility cells" developed by the consultant and the parent.

As a general principle, real problems and relative problems require parenting plus plans. Situational problems and value problems are ordinarily quite appropriate for and responsive to good parenting. In addition, problems in the top three rows are more common to early elementary age and preschool-age children, while problems in the bottom three rows are more common to older grade school age children and adolescents.

Problem Dimension and Type

What is the definition of the problem? ______________________________

Dimension	*Real Problem*	*Relative Problem*	*Situational Problem*	*Value Problem*
Physical/Doing				
Emotional/Feeling				
Moral/Spiritual				
Social/Interpersonal				
Sexual/Sensual				
Intellectual/Cognitive				

ACTIVITY 13

PARENTING ASSESSMENT

THIS ACTIVITY samples several areas of parenting in order to draw attention to those areas that are going well and those where there are some problems. As with other interpersonal areas, the key is to spend most parenting time and energy emphasizing those areas that are working, those things that are going well. At the same time, some effort and consultation activity need to focus in those areas that are working less well. Using a rating scale from five to one, rate yourself in terms of the statements below. Five equals almost always, four equals usually, three equals sometimes, two equals seldom, and one equals almost never.

Once you have completed your ratings for each item, add your ratings together and divide the total by fourteen. This will give you a parenting score. Generally, effective parent/child relationships are found where the parenting score is 4.0 or higher. Even when a score is achieved at this level, though, attention needs to be given to those areas where individual item ratings are three or less and especially where the ratings are two or less. When parent/child difficulties arise, the first and best strategy is to go back to this activity, focus on each item, and then work on being sure that the parenting score stays in higher than 4.0 for at least a month or so.

___ 1. I am reasonable and fair when discipling my child.
___ 2. I know what my child needs and what is important to him/her.
___ 3. I am able to get my child to cooperate with me.
___ 4. I spend time with my child everyday.
___ 5. My child likes to spend time with me.
___ 6. I am pleased with and proud of my child.
___ 7. I am familiar with and interested in my child's activities.

____ 8. I know about and am helping with my child's problems and difficulties.
____ 9. I set a good example for my child.
____10. I give my child his/her space.
____11. My child and I regularly talk with each other.
____12. I am interested in my child's ideas and thoughts about things.
____13. I support and encourage my child's being who he/she is and his/her unique style.
____14. I am a good parent.

DISCUSSION

The items in the activity blend and combine to suggest what might be thought of as parenting themes. The first of these themes relates to the client's knowing what her child needs and what is important to the child. This combines with being familiar with and interested in the child's activities and involvements. The blending continues with knowing about and helping with the child's problems and difficulties. In addition, the parent interest extends to the youngster's ideas and thoughts about things, his perceptions and point of view. The principle is that being a good parent means that, as a parent, "know your child" is the first order of business.

The second theme combines spending time with the child each day and being sure that the parent and the child talk with each other regularly. This is, of course, a minimum condition for knowing the child. The principle encourages the parent to "Be available to your child."

The third theme blends being someone with whom the child likes to spend time and being pleased with and proud of the child. These two factors in turn blend with setting a good example for the youngster into a cluster of parent characteristics to which the young person can easily relate and with which she may identify. The relationship is with someone with whom the youngster is comfortable and is a relationship within which the young person may easily participate. This ease of participation is facilitated by the parent's giving the young person her space where she is supported in being who she is. The principle is to develop and maintain a positive and open relationship with the child.

Developing and maintaining an open and positive relationship with the child where the parent both knows the child and is available to her incorporates most of what is involved in being a good parent. Within this type of parent/child environment, getting the child to cooperate will be relatively easy and will happen relatively spontaneously. Why does the child cooperate? Because she sees the parent as someone who reciprocates cooperation and as someone with whom it is nice to cooperate.

Discipline is still necessary but is, within this context, a relatively minor part of the parenting task. Parents need to exercise parental authority as will be discussed in the next activity. The only requirement is that the exercise of that authority—discipline—is reasonable and fair. The consultant will want to encourage the parent to talk with the youngster about the reasonableness and fairness of discipline, especially if the young person is of grade school age or older. In addition, the consultant will want to review the parent's discipline primarily focusing on the extent to which that discipline is both reasonable and fair.

For example, reasonable discipline is nonviolent, characterized by gentle firmness, is proportional to the difficulty or transgression, is reasonably consistent, and takes into consideration the age of the child and the specific situation in which the child was involved. Fairness also takes into consideration these factors and looks at the simple principle of equity among and between siblings, whether or not any discipline was appropriate on a particular occasion, and the extent to which discipline is carried out in an even-handed way.

An important point needs emphasis. Negative discipline or punishment should never be a reaction to something the child did or did not do. Punishment should never be retaliatory or represent some form of retribution. Discipline has a simple purpose: to decrease the likelihood of unacceptable behavior in the future and to increase the likelihood of appropriate behavior. In this sense, discipline is always for the sake of the future and is never a response to things that have happened in the past.

Following from the above thought, discipline is and ought to be nothing more or less than a significant educational experience for the young person. It is in the interest of her learning. As a learning opportunity and as an educational experience, discipline should always be understood as a positive intervention in the interest of the child's future behavior and well being. Forcing children into compliance, then, is never appropriate. The goal is to teach them more appropriate, more acceptable, more effective behavior. From this perspective, the teaching tips in part one of this book apply.

Occasionally, discipline involves the impostition of negative consequences. The youngster's environment is adjusted in ways that result in some behavior leading to unwanted or undesirable consequences. These negative consequences should be such that they simply encourage the youngster to adopt more appropriate, more acceptable behavior in the future. The next activity relates to the use of authority in relationship to negative consequences.

An additional point about discipline is in order. Parents will get about the same results using either a permissive or autocratic approach to discipline. The key is being reasonably consistent with the approach. The worst results will be found with parents who vacillate between autocratic and permissive approaches: vacillate between cracking down and giving up. The problematic effect is compounded when one parent is fairly permissive while the other is fairly autocratic. Consistency as noted here also includes both parents being consistent relative to the approach being used.

The best results will be obtained using what has been called an authoritative approach to parenting. In this situation, both parents are reasonably consistent and both have fairly clear rules, fairly clear expectations, and a fairly clear pattern of dealing with significant variations from expectations. In this sense, the approach is toward the autocratic end of the continuum. The additional factor is one of talking with the child about the problem, explaining the reasons for discipline, and, to the extent possible, being sure that the child understands what is happening and why. No, it is not necessary that she agrees. It is only important that she understands. (Note) It is important to use the same approach with infants and toddlers and with older children, even though they may not understand the discussions and explanations. Even in these situations, an attitude of talking, discussing, and explaining is conveyed nonverbally.

THE HEART OF PARENTING

Our own child is special to us. He or she is part of our being. This is true whether the child is our biological offspring or has become our child as a result of special circumstances. If we do not hold this special feeling with sincerity and enthusiasm, the child will know and will suffer in proportion.

Most interaction with our children has little if anything to do with encouragement or discouragement, boundaries or limits; rather, we participate with them in the fun and frustration of being parents and kids physically, emotionally, and socially. We want them to love us, to love themselves, to love other people, and to love the world around them. We express our love through touching, physical involvement, playing, doing things together, sharing feelings and fears and frustrations, going places with them and wanting them to go places with us, and allowing them the freedom to grow and to experience the world away from us. Our relationship with them is not exclusive. We want them to have an exciting life of their own, knowing that their relationship with us is secure and predictable. In addition, we want our children to respect us, to respect themselves, other people, and the world about them. Much of a child's attitude toward herself and toward the world about her comes from our attitudes about her.

Fortunately or unfortunately, many children do not turn out like their parents. Why does this happen? Very simply, it happens because parents are not the only influence on children, albeit the primary influence. Just as children learn to love by being loved, they learn respect for self and others by being respected. Our behavior, attitudes, and beliefs will be reflected in our children. More than we may ever know, they "do as we do."

Children also develop attitudes toward themselves and others as a response to the attitudes and beliefs others communicate to them about themselves. In part, children become what we tell them they will become. We convey this definition of self through our physical, emotional, and social interaction with them as well as through the way we relate as parenting adults. Beyond these things, there is a whole world of influences over which we have little control. Our hope must be that we have encouraged and discouraged their capacities so they can effectively deal with the multiple influences of the world. We hope our loving respect has been strong enough and clear enough to be integrated into their being as they move out into a world which may not perceive them as unique. Their sense of being special comes from us. We can only hope it is solid enough to last a lifetime.

ACTIVITY 14

PARENT AUTHORITY APPROACH

CONSIDER EACH of the seven authority approaches below (1-7). Look at your own parenting style and think about how often you use each of these approaches. Which one do you use the most? Rank it number one. The approach used next most often should be ranked as number two, with the approach used least often ranked as number seven. The result will be a ranking from most used to least used in terms of your approach to the exercise of authority with your children.

Once you have completed ranking the seven approaches in terms of how frequently you actually use them, go back and rank the seven in terms of what you think would be ideal in terms of the use of the seven approaches. Now compare the authority mix you actually use to what you think would be ideal. Also, take time to discuss the rankings and the difference between actual and ideal rankings with your consultant.

1. TITLE AUTHORITY. Children are told that they should or should not do things because you—their parent—said so. Your title—parent—gives you the right to tell them what to do or what not to do.
2. REWARD/PUNISHMENT AUTHORITY. If they submit to or go along with what you want or say, you will reward them in some positive way. If they do not, you will punish them.
3. REFERENT AUTHORITY. You present to them ideas of right and wrong, good and bad, and encourage them to conform to these standards. Sometimes this takes the form of encouraging certain behavior because this is "what we do" in our family or is consistent with what our family believes.

4. THE VOICE OF EXPERIENCE. You base your demands, expectations, and suggestions on your personal experience with the same or similar situation. "When I was young, . . ." is a typical intro to the voice of experience. Another similar approach starts with, "When you have lived as long as I have, you will. . . ." The idea is that your experience takes precedence over the perceptions and judgements of the young person.
5. INFORMATIONAL AUTHORITY. Your authority is based on your having knowledge or information that the young person does not possess. This authority approach is also in operation when you encourage the young person to read the instructions, talk with someone who knows about that sort of thing, or go to the library to find more information. The same authority approach is being used when you encourage the young person to check with his teacher, talk to a professional to learn the facts, or to wait awhile until you or the young person can find out more about the situation.
6. CONTROL OF RESOURCES AND OPPORTUNITIES. This approach is ordinarily being used when youngsters are given allowances, when privileges are given or withheld, when special arrangements are made for things like lessons or the opportunity to participate in special events, or when you are trying to influence the behavior of the young person by controlling resources or opportunities. This naturally includes things like driving privileges, using the family car, grounding the young person, sending young children to bed early, and so on.
7. ACCEPTANCE/REJECTION AUTHORITY. This approach is used far more than many parents realize. Acceptance is being given anytime you give the young person a special hug, smile at her, say nice things either to the young person or to other people about the youngster, or in some way reflect your approval and affirmation. Also, acceptance authority is being used when you reflect a continuing caring and love for the young person even when she gets into trouble, does something of which you disapprove, or behaves outside of the boundaries of family norms and expectations. Conversely, you are rejecting the young person when you become angry with her, send her to her room, do not talk to her or give the youngster the "cold shoulder," or in other ways let the young person know that you are displeased, do not feel very good about her right now, or are unhappy with the young person. An important part of this authority approach is to devote the time and sensitivity required to know when in fact you are using it.

DISCUSSION

The activity presents seven approaches to authority which good parents blend and mix as they relate to and interact with their youngsters. Referent authority is almost always a part of the exercise of authority when using the authoritative approach to discipline discussed in the last activity. The authoritative approach also relies heavily on "the voice of experience" and informational authority as explained in this activity. Continuing to relate the current activity to the last activity, reward/punishment authority and control of resources and opportunities are generally the form in which negative discipline is seen when negative discipline is used as part of a learning experience for a child.

The consultant will want to first work with parents in terms of recognizing and minimizing their use of acceptance/rejection authority. In fact, most parents would be well advised if they were to avoid the use of this type of authority as much as possible. Within the relationship with the parent, the child will naturally and spontaneously feel acceptance. When the parent becomes upset, frustrated, annoyed, or displeased with the child, the child will feel rejected and pushed away to some extent, whether this is what the parent intends or not. Since the negative effect of acceptance/rejection authority is going to be experienced by the child in any event, the parent should avoid its use anytime that is possible. The consultant will need to work in the educational area with the parent to increase awareness of and consciousness of those things which are experienced by children as rejection. These behaviors, attitudes, and approaches are, then, those which need minimizing.

At the next level, parents and the consultant should work together to reduce the extent to which parents use title authority. "You will do that because I am your parent and because I said so." If attention will return to the discussion of authoritative discipline raised in the last activity, one can easily see that this approach to authority is inconsistence with the authoritative approach to discipline. "Being the parent" may be the source of the parent's right to direct the child and of the parent's power to see to it that directions are followed. It is, nonetheless, not an adequate reason or sufficient explanation. In fact, if better reasons and explanations are not available, it may be that discipline or the use of authority are not reasonable or appropriate on that occasion. Interestingly, the child already knows who the parent is and knows about the parent's authority. Simply iterating the obvious to the child does not extend her knowledge or understanding.

The remaining five approaches to authority mix and blend into two main themes. First, the use of reward/punishment authority and authority based on controlling resources and opportunities combine into what might be thought of as a negative discipline theme. These are approaches used by good parents primarily for the purpose of controlling their youngsters. The second theme combines referent authority with "the voice of experience" and informational authority into a pattern of positive discipline or a pattern of influencing youngsters. The two themes interplay to limit and control the youngster on the one hand and to influence and direct the young person on the other hand.

From a developmental perspective, the first theme is very visible and present in good parenting relationships with younger children, although nearly absent in the parent/child interaction with adolescents. Alternatively, the second theme—positive discipline—is the major authority theme with older children and adolescents and is seen as an approximately equal theme with negative discipline in relationships with younger children.

As can be seen, the authority mix depends a lot on the individual child but also depends more generally on the developmental age of the youngster. Parents are beginning to get into trouble if the mix is not gradually shifting in favor of positive discipline over time. This is especially true if negative discipline is a major theme with older children and adolescents. In fact, negative discipline begins to become completely inappropriate for older adolescents. They are simply at a stage in their lives where the exercise of parental power and control are inappropriate and generally ineffective.

ACTIVITY 15

CHILDREN'S PARENTING ASSESSMENT

THIS ACTIVITY basically follows the same idea as was used in the parenting assessment activity except that it looks at the parent/child relationship from the young person's point of view. It will assist youngsters in thinking about the various areas and responsibilities involved in parenting and facilitate their developing a more understanding sense of how tough it really is to be a parent. Also, it will enable the young person to more clearly explain to his/her parent those things which the young person is finding most problematic or difficult within the parent/child relationship.

When there are difficulties in the parent/child relationship, it will be helpful for the parent to complete the parenting assessment activity and for the young person to complete this activity. They may then compare and talk about their ratings.

Use a rating scale from five to one: five equals almost always, four equals usually, three equals sometimes, two equals seldom, and one equals almost never. When you are finished rating each statement, add the ratings together and divide the total by fifteen. The result is a youngster's parenting score. Generally, a score of 4.0 or higher is found in mutually satisfying and effective parent/child relationships.

MY PARENT

___ 1. Is reasonable and fair when disciplining me.
___ 2. Understands what I need and what is important to me.
___ 3. Is able to get me to cooperate.
___ 4. Spends time with me.
___ 5. Is someone with whom I like to spend time.
___ 6. Is interested in my activities.

___ 7. Knows about and is helping me with my problems and difficulties.
___ 8. Is pleased with and proud of me.
___ 9. Gives me my space.
___10. Sets a good example for me.
___11. Takes time to talk with me.
___12. Is interested in my ideas and in what I think about things.
___13. Sticks up for me when I am right.
___14. Lets me be me.
___15. Is a good parent.

DISCUSSION

This activity is used in conjunction with the earlier parenting assessment activity. It is essentially the same activity, looking at the parent/child relationship from the youngster's point of view. The consultant will want to maintain the perspective of the parenting principles and themes developed in the earlier activity when working with young people in the context of this activity.

As an extended use of the activity, the consultant may want to work with the young person in developing a list of ideas or perceptions to share with his parents. In terms as specific as possible, in what ways does the youngster think his parent is unreasonable when disciplining him? What are some examples of unreasonableness? Similarly, in what ways does the young person think the parent is being unfair? What are some examples of unfairness? Important to this process is the next step, however. What does the youngster think would be more reasonable—more fair?

What does the youngster perceive his needs to be? Within this range of perceived needs, which ones do the parents understand and which ones do they not understand? How would the young person know if his parents did understand the youngster's needs? The same approach may be used to focus on what is important to the young person. The process then extends to the parents' knowing about the youngster's problems and difficulties and helping with them. What would be helpful? How would you know if your parents were helping?

The consultant may also help the youngster in understanding that the parent/child relationship is a reciprocal opportunity for both the youngster and the parent. Does the youngster spend time with the parent? What does he do to facilitate spending more time with the parent? Does the youngster make an effort to be someone with whom the parent would want to spend time? Does the young person make an effort to talk with the parent openly and honestly? Along with the youngster's assessing the parent/child relationship in terms of the parent, he needs also to assess the relationship in terms of his participation in the relationship.

Is the young person able to get the parent to cooperate? Again, the principle of reciprocity applies. An important element here is being someone with whom the parent is pleased and of whom the parent is proud. These are characteristics that lead to the young person's being more attractive to the parent. What does the child think there is about him that should bring pleasure to the parent? What is there about him in which the parent may take pride? The youngster will find that attention to these traits and characteristics will have the positive effect of increasing the extent to which the parent cooperates with him.

Having their space is important to young people. At the same time, though, they need to set an example first by giving the parent his space and by being an individual with whom the parent is comfortable in a relationship where the child is given his space given who the child is from the parent's point of view. "What is there about you, about the example that you set that should encourage your parent to give you the space, freedom, and independent opportunity you want? In what ways do you set an example of someone who has earned these opportunities and privileges?"

The same processes may be used in reference to the other variables in the activity. Once the young person has completed the activity and has dealt with the ideas and issues raised in the discussion section, it is time to process all of the materials with his parent. In highly functional families, the young person will probably be able to do this on an independent basis. Where parent/child relationships are somewhat more problematic, however, this is probably best handled in a joint session including both the youngster and the parents with the consultant. If the youngster is able, it is best for him to directly raise and discuss each of the pieces with his parents, with the consultant's serving a supportive and facilitating role. If the youngster finds this difficult, however, the consultant may bring up the materials with the parent, taking the role of the young person. Even in this situation, though, it is extremely important that the young person is present both to own and accept responsibility for the materials and to have the benefit of the modeling being demonstrated by the consultant. Over time, the young person needs to take the more active role.

ACTIVITY 16

DEVELOPMENTAL PARENTING

THIS ACTIVITY is intended for parents and may be used either as an outline for single presentations to groups or as a topic guide for parenting classes. In addition, it may be used as an adjunct to counseling situations with parents and families. The goal of the activity is first to introduce the idea of the multidimensionality of children and the importance of understanding and relating to the whole child. The second goal is to encourage an orientation to the needs and interests of the growing and developing child and away from seeing parenting as something one correctly or incorrectly does to children. The third goal is to encourage an approach that emphasizes the relational, interpersonal basis of parent/child interaction and discourages any emphasis on direct control or use of direct power within the parent/child interaction.

THE MULTIDIMENSIONAL CHILD

1. Your child is a physical/doing person. What do you do to facilitate and encourage his/her healthy physical growth and development?
2. Your child is an emotional/feeling person. What do you do to facilitate and encourage his/her healthy emotional growth and development?
3. Your child is a moral/spiritual person. What do you do to facilitate and encourage his/her healthy moral growth and development?
4. Your child is a social/interpersonal person. What do you do to facilitate and encourage his/her healthy social growth and development, healthy interpersonal involvements and activities?
5. Your child is a sexual person. What do you do to facilitate and encourage his/her healthy sexual growth and development, healthy sexual experience?

6. Your child is a cognitive/thinking person. What do you do to facilitate and encourage his/her healthy and ongoing cognitive growth and development?
7. Your child is part of his/her environment. What do you do to facilitate and encourage a positive environment for your child at home, at school, in your community?

BEING PARENTS AND CHILDREN TOGETHER

The key to being the parent the child needs comes in terms of understanding and responding to the unique child while maintaining the balance between overinvolvement and underinvolvement, exercising too much control and providing inadequate structure and guidance, influencing too much and not enough, overparenting and underparenting. The next key comes in terms of modifying and adjusting one's parental behavior and parenting style in ways that are responsive to the development and changing interests of the child from infancy into adulthood.

8. How do you manage your child's environment in ways that take into consideration where he/she is developmentally? What did you do differently when the child was younger? What will you do differently when he/she is older?
9. In what ways does your approach emphasize controlling the child and in what ways does it emphasize controlling the child's environment, the child's opportunities?
10. (Including verbal techniques) How do you maximize the use of positive physical techniques—reinforcements—and minimize or eliminate the use of negative physical techniques—punishment—as you influence and manage the child? How do you adjust these techniques to take into account the age of the child?
11. How do you relate to your child emotionally and use his/her sense of attachment to you as you influence and manage the child? To what extent is the appeal in terms of doing it for you or because you asked? To what extent is your approach based on your being happy or upset and to what extent is it based on what the child sees as being or not being in his/her self-interest?
12. In what ways does your approach to the moral development of your child emphasize rewards and punishment—conditioning—and in what ways does it emphasize simple reasoning, judgment, and an

internalized sense of right and wrong, good and bad? In what ways is your approach different for preschool-aged children, grade school-aged children, adolescents, adult children?

13. As your child relates to peers and is involved in other social relationships, how do you use permission and restriction as a way of influencing those involvements? In what ways do you encourage positive involvements and discourage negative involvements? How does your approach take into consideration the age of the child, where the child is developmentally?
14. In what ways does your approach encourage and facilitate the blending of physical, emotional, moral, and social development into the developing sexual interests and involvements of the young person? To what extent does your approach emphasize controlling the sexual activities and involvements of the young person and to what extent does it emphasize faith in the child and in his/her judgment, discrimination, and ability to manage himself/herself?
15. How do you facilitate and encourage the cognitive development of the child? To what extent does your approach emphasize the child's adopting your values, beliefs, and ways of thinking about things and to what extent does it emphasize his/her independent and developing judgment, reasoning, decision making, and thinking? How do you assure congruence between your approach and the developmental level of the child?
16. As the child moves from childhood into adolescence, how does your parenting approach take into consideration: your increasing inability to physically control the young person, the increasing reality that limit-setting only works if the young person consents to the limits, the continuing need to influence the behavior and actions of the young person, the decreasing appeal to the young person of doing things for you and the increasing need for him/her to do things for himself/herself, the increasing moral and value-related influence of peers and society, and the young person's growing autonomy?
17. How do you use discussion and informational support within your relationship with the young person, knowing that receptivity to these techniques is at the young person's discretion?
18. What do you do to maintain a position where you may provide the young person consultation, advice, and guidance on an as needed basis while maximizing the likelihood that the young person will take advantage of these resources available from you?

19. What are you doing now to encourage and facilitate your adult children to maintain a relationship with you within which you may: extend physical support and advice, provide emotional nurturance and understanding, convey moral respect, be involved both as parent and friend, demonstrate acceptance of who they are sexually, and serve as consultant and sounding board?

PART FOUR

BEING MARRIED WITH STYLE, ALL THE TIME, ON PURPOSE

INTRODUCTION

THE INTERNAL TRIANGLE

IF WE THINK in terms of there being three major dimensions within a healthy and successful marriage relationship, we can understand these dimensions as including; being FRIENDS, being PARTNERS, and being LOVERS. The diagram graphically presents the idea.

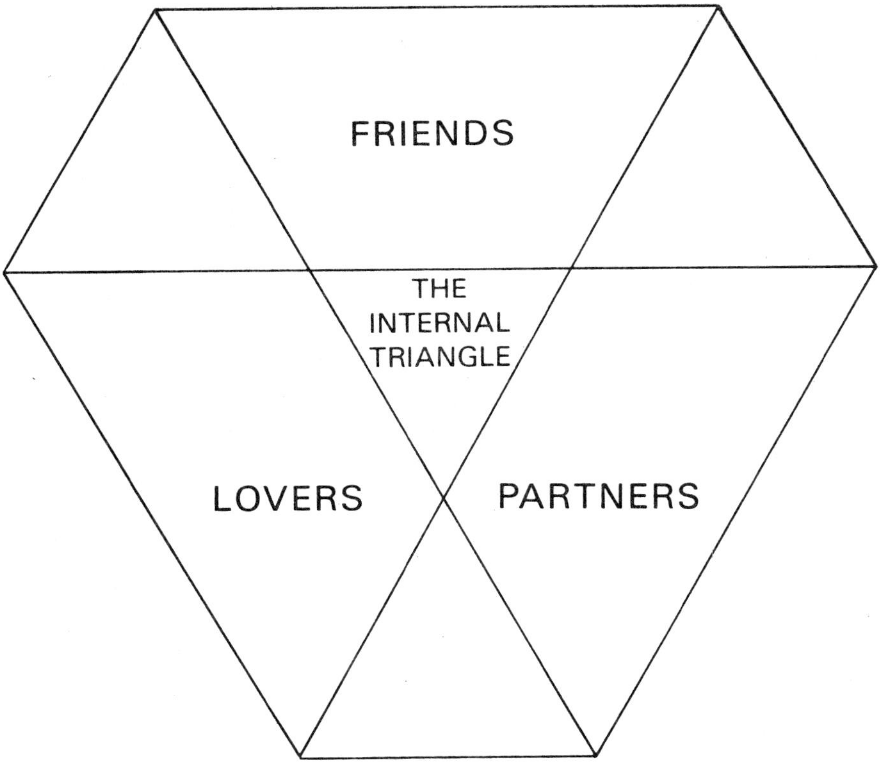

FRIENDS–PARTNERS–LOVERS: Life in the Internal Triangle

Using the figure as a conceptual guide, we can see that people who are successfully involved in a marriage relationship are friends. We then need to think about the friendship aspect of any marriage relationship as part of our assessment and understanding. We also see that successfully married people are partners in the sense that they work together financially, as parents, and in other ways. Marriage-positive people involved in an ongoing marriage relationship are also successful and satisfied lovers who voluntarily restrict their sexual activity to their relationship.

In addition to the three core dimensions, we also see that the core areas overlap and blend with each other, as we understand the figure as a whole as representing the marriage and understand that the partners occupy different locations in the figure at different times. Our sampling needs to take this into consideration as do our consultation activities with the partners.

What makes the marriage relationship unique and different from other relationships? It is the internal triangle. The uniqueness and importance to the individuals of marriage comes in terms of the blending and merger of the core dimensions as seen diagrammatically in the internal triangle. This may be thought of as the heart of the marriage. Understanding the significance of the internal triangle also makes it easy to see why marriages only work well when all three core dimensions are working well individually and are working well in concert with each other.

When using the educational approach, it is important to first assess the marriage relationship and to interpret that assessment in terms of the core dimensions and their interactions with each other. Educational, "How to" attention then focuses on how the partner can exhibit increased and more effective friendship behavior, increased and more effective partner behavior, and increased and more effective lover behavior.

Specific behavioral techniques that you want to teach or encourage should be specific and translatable into how, what, where, and when. This approach can be reinforced by use of the feel-felt-found technique discussed earlier and the RECIPES approach already discussed.

PERSPECTIVE DEVELOPMENT— THE US BOX CONTINUED

As you work with people in conflicted and crisis relationships, it is important to help them maintain focus on the goal of building a new relationship, while avoiding the trap of trying to repair the old one. The focus is on building a new US box. It is important to see that the goal is not to change the individuals, building either a new ME box or a new YOU box. They simply need to focus their attention on building a new US box. They say to you, "But we will both have to change." No. That notion should be put under the heading of "an old wives' tale." The old adage says that when a relationship goes bad, both people will have to change. This is not only silly but also quite unlikely. As individuals, people usually do not change very much, and then only grudgingly because they feel they have to. They may behave a little differently. They may slightly modify some of their habits, reactions, demands, expectations, and so on. But they are, nevertheless, the same people—relatively unchanged, but growing. It is not unusual, after a crisis experience, to talk with people who indicate that things are much better, their new relationships are more satisfying, but they are the same as they have always been. "I don't feel any different. I am the same as I always was. It's the new relationship that's different. That's what makes the difference."

Individuals who are involved in the process of building a new US box must agree that, as individuals, they are each all right. They will not, and do not really want to, change each other. They only want to build a new US box. Recall that the building process adds bits to the relationship. If one of the builders thinks that the other one is not all right, he will add many bad bits to the US box about the other person. As these bad bits accumulate, the new US box will begin to deteriorate. Similarly, if either individual has been forced to make substantial changes or life adjustments, he or she will gradually resent the pressure and use of force. Bad bits related to this resentment will begin to slip into the US box, causing it to go bad. To begin an US box, both people must agree.

1. I am all right the way I am.
2. You are all right the way you are.
3. We are going to build an ongoing, ongrowing US box that is acceptable to both of us.

As you work with people involved in conflicted or crisis relationships, if it becomes apparent that they will not agree to these three basic rules of US box building, you should refuse to take the process any further and should encourage them, as individuals, to save their energy and emotions for other times and other people.

Mike and Mary have reached a point of crisis in their marriage. You ask: How can I help? Mike answers: Our marriage is on the rocks. We have three small children who deserve a normal family. We have to get things back together for their sake. You ask: How do you see the situation, Mary? Mary: I agree. There's nothing that's going to help our relationship, but at least we have to learn to be civilized for those kids. You say: You both seem to feel pretty hopeless about your marriage. What good do you think it will do to talk with me about it? Mike answers: You can make her understand that she has to stay home and take care of those kids. She can't be always running around and spending all of her time over at the neighbors', drinking coffee or whatever they do. She has responsibilities at home, and I expect her to do them. Mary: Don't talk to me about responsibilities. It's not me that's going out all the time, coming home drunk, acting like a wild man in front of the kids. Mike: Get off my back! I married you, didn't I? Don't I go to work every day and pay the bills? You have more than a lot of people. I never told you I'd love you. I told you I'd do what's right by you. I married you, didn't I? Mary, beginning to cry: Yes, and I wish you hadn't. I didn't love you then and I don't now. I can't stand you. Mike: You might as well stop that. It's not going to do you a damn bit of good. I told you with the first one I'd help you raise it. I'm not sure the other two are mine, but I told you I'd help you raise them, too. You can just get off that stuff and quit acting like a little hurt puppy. Mary: But I never thought it would be this way. I thought maybe we'd get something worked out, and things might really be okay. Mike: Things are okay, if you'd just quit acting like they were supposed to be something they aren't. You say: Neither of you seems to feel very good about the other one. Mike: She knew what the deal was. I don't feel any different about her than I ever did. I told her I'd do what's right, and I'm doing it. Mary: I know, but I don't know whether I'll be able to go on this way or not. I can't deal with it this way much longer. It's getting to me. Mike: Then get out, but if you go, you're sure not taking those kids. Mary: I can't leave the kids. You know that. Mike says to you: That's where it is. That's where it always ends up. She threatens to leave, and I tell her she's not taking the kids, and she says she's not leaving without them. It just always ends up there. That's not good for me or for her, and especially it's not good for the kids. What are you going to do about it? You say: It's not my problem. The problem belongs to you and Mary and the kids. The question is, what are *you* going to do about it? Mike: I don't know. That's why we're here. You say to Mary: What do you think you will do about the situation, Mary? Mary: I don't know.

A CARING PROCESS

Only when both individuals are at the starting point—each agreeing that the other is all right and that they are going to build an US box with care and concern—are they ready to build a new relationship. Now, how do they build an US box? The *how* of it is fairly simple. The *doing* of it is extremely difficult and requires much time and caring. First, they will each encourage and promote all of those things involved in the life process. Similarly, they will discourage and avoid anything and everything that interferes with the life process. Basically, this means that they will each, as individuals, recognize, respect, and encourage the other person, and that they each can and should expect and receive respect and encouragement from the other. Each person should say, "My ME box is mine, and you stay out of it; only with my permission can you interfere with it. If you keep this part of the bargain, I will do the same for you. We each have our own lives, our own interests, thoughts, and ideas, and that is good. Our US box is only a part of our lives."

When a baby is born, he has almost no ME box. He is almost totally involved in an US box he shares with his mother. As he matures, he gradually develops a ME box, and in turn, his ME box becomes involved in many US boxes. This growing and becoming is central to his life process. As people build an US box, they must recognize and remember that they each have their own individual life process. Although it is hard to do, children need to see that their parents are growing and becoming, that they have their own life processes. In any important and close relationship, whether it be between children, between children and adults, or between adults, recognition and encouragement of the life process is critical. As people begin the US box building process, their contract starts with:

1. We recognize, accept, and will encourage our individual life processes, our growing and becoming as separate and distinct people.
2. We will avoid interfering with or trying to change each other's life process. That way we can devote our time, energy, and caring to the growing and becoming of our relationship—its life process.

The central point for both people to accept is that they are, as individuals, growing and becoming and that their relationship—their US box—must keep pace. If it does not, their bad relationship will continue, and their US box cannot grow. If they can start at that point, they then need to develop some way of deciding what bits get into their relationship and what bits stay out. As they start to build their new US box, they must necessarily start with no bits. This is extremely difficult and emphasizes the importance of starting a new relationship instead of trying to fix or repair the old one. As you work with individuals in the beginning stage of the US box process, you will want to help them become alert to assumptions, ideas, beliefs, feelings, attitudes, and so on, that they are trying to carry over from their old relationship. It will be very easy for them to subconsciously or unintentionally use bits from the old relationship without agreeing about whether or not these bits can go into the new relationship. They will need to come up with some process or set of rules about how bits get added to or dropped out of their new relationship. Although, ideally, every bit should be discussed and evaluated before it is added to the relationship, this is not really possible. Both individuals will subconsciously or unintentionally put bits into the relationship, and you, despite your best efforts, will not be able to recognize and pick up on every bit going into the relationship. It is important, then, for the individuals to have a way of confronting each other about bits that seem to be in the relationship. Those bits needing discussion are usually feelings, perceptions, judgments, expectations, and so on, that seem to have slipped into the relationship without discussion or recognition. The rule is, of course, that any important bit put into the US box by one individual can only be put in if he tells the other person about it. If we are building an US box and I have a bit that says that you are pretty, smart, unfair, lazy, too rough, bad tempered, too skinny, make extra work for me, or any of a million other minor to major important bits, I have to tell you about it in some way before I can put it in our US box. At the same rate, if you have a feeling or belief that I have put an important bit in the US box without letting you know in some way, you have a right and responsibility to confront me on that. At that point, we will discuss the particular belief, thought, idea, notion, and so forth, to decide whether or not it will stay in the relationship.

In addition, you may have some important bits about yourself that you want in the US box. You may want me to believe and understand things like: you like me, you don't like messy cars, you get angry when I come home late, you have a problem falling asleep and don't appreciate my getting up and making a lot of noise right after you have gone to bed, and so on, until you have included all those things you want me to know, think, and believe about you. Parents and children, husbands and wives, friends, and so on, will need to develop a way of letting each other know what bits are being put into the US box as well as what bits about themselves they would like put in the US box.

We can think of some important bits that usually go into US boxes. Only the extremes have been listed, but each of the bits comes in a lot of forms and varieties. The list is, of course, neither all inclusive nor exhaustive. It is only intended to be suggestive and that it may stimulate your thinking about kinds of important feelings, thoughts, beliefs, ideas, and so on, that typically go into US boxes.

YOU ARE:

pretty — ugly
loving — cold
smart — dumb
happy — sad
fun to be with — not fun to be with
fair — unfair
gentle — rough
reasonable — unreasonable
ambitious — lazy
considerate — selfish

As individuals become involved in the US box building process, they add literally thousands of bits to their relationship. In addition to this process of adding bits to the relationship, however, they need to develop rules and agreements about the process of dropping bits from the relationship. For example, "I thought you weren't trying, but now I think you are." . . . "I was annoyed with your sleeping so much, but now I understand that you really are tired." . . . "I was upset with you, but I am not upset with you now." . . . "I thought you were a responsible person, but I do not think so anymore." . . . "I thought you were the kind of person who would lie to me, but I do not believe that anymore." Bits that get tossed out of the relationship of course may be very important or may be fairly unimportant. Both individuals need to know, though, when bits are being tossed out. As they think about building their new US box, they have already agreed to recognize, encourage, and not to interfere with each other's life process, while working on their relationship's growing and becoming. Now their contract needs to expand to include further agreements about the building process. They continue with:

3. We can only add bits to our US box after we have in some way let the other person know about it.
4. We each have some bits about ourselves that we want added to the US box, and it is our responsibility to let the other person know about those bits.

5. If we feel that a bit has been added to the US box without discussion or understanding, it is our responsibility to confront the other person about this; and it is his responsibility to discuss the bit.
6. If either of us is going to toss a bit out of the relationship, we have the responsibility to let the other person know what we are going to do, and we both have a responsibility to discuss it with each other.

Following their agreements about the life process and building process, the individuals need to develop some understanding and agreements about the meaning/valuing process. They must develop some understanding about things like: what's good, what's bad; what's important, what's not important; what's necessary, what isn't necessary; what's acceptable, what's not acceptable; what's fair, what's unfair; which things have to do with love and caring, which things are not related to love and caring. In most relationships, one of the greatest sources of conflict is over the meaning and value placed on elements in the relationship. For example, a husband and wife both agree that the husband is overweight. He thinks this is an extremely undesirable thing and wants to make every effort to lose the weight. She thinks being a little overweight is healthy and gets angry with him when he tries to diet.

Another example, a teenager agrees to be home at 11:00 P.M. His parents think this is an extremely important agreement and that it should be kept very specifically. The teenager does not think it is a particularly important agreement and felt that it wouldn't matter so long as he was home by 11:30. When he came in at 11:25, there was a rather heated argument. For the bits in the US box, both individuals agreed to put them there. But it is quite possible, however, that they may not be placing the same meaning or value on those bits in the US box. That can cause conflict and confusion. As they build their new US box, they will want to give special attention to the meaning/valuing process.

Nancy and Paul have been dating for a few weeks. Their physical relationship had been fairly mild, mostly at Paul's insistence. Nancy could not understand Paul's reluctance and teased him about it one evening when they were alone. After they had teased and joked about it for a while, Paul became more relaxed, and he and Nancy enjoyed being more intimate. Soon after that evening, Nancy started seeing Paul less and less. Even though she did not want to go out with him as often, they both enjoyed the greater intimacy when they did go out. Paul is very conflicted, though. He cannot understand why she does not want to see him more, since he thought the "bit" calling for greater intimacy meant that Nancy loved him. The increased intimacy did not have anything like this meaning or value for Nancy. She saw it as pleasant, fun, and something to do when she went out with Paul. This difference in meaning and valuing created a lot of misunderstanding and conflict in their relationship. Had they been able to discuss the meaning/valuing of the bit before adding it to their relationship, Paul could have avoided the hurt and anxiety, and Nancy could have avoided having to deal with Paul's confusing and puzzling behavior.

Mr. P has to work very long hours and can't spend much time with his son. They both have a bit in their US box that says "Dad has to work long hours." When they are together, they really enjoy each other's company, have a very good time, can laugh and play or sit quietly and talk seriously. Mr. P is, however, very concerned about not being able to spend more time with his son. He thinks that this will cause his son to have difficulty as he grows and develops. He feels that "deep down inside" his son really resents him. When Mr. P is working, he frequently thinks about this quite a lot, feels very guilty, and worries. His son, on the contrary, feels very good about his dad and understands that he has to work long hours. His son feels that his dad is working such long hours for the benefit of him, his mother, and the other children. He feels that his dad is really doing something for them when he is working. From the son's point of view, his dad is interested in him and pays a lot of attention to him when he can. When his dad is working, he is doing it out of love and interest in the son and the rest of the family. Rather than harboring resentment for his dad, the son has nothing but good, positive feelings. The problem is, of course, with the meaning or valuing of the bit "Dad has to work long hours" when it was put in their US box. This difference in valuing and meaning is causing the father unnecessary guilt and worry.

It is apparent that the meaning/valuing process is an important part of US box building. The individuals must, then, extend their contract to include agreements about the meaning/valuing process:

7. We will be specific about the meaning and value placed on bits in the US box.
8. We will agree on the meaning and value given to any important bit before placing it in the US box.
9. We will add no bit to the US box unless we can agree on a common meaning and value. As a rule of thumb, if we disagree, we will only add the bit to the US box if we can agree to give it the least significant meaning and lowest value held by either of us.

Finally, both individuals have some notions or ideas about what the US box should be like, what it can be like, and what it should not be like. They have some notions about what kinds of bits belong in the US box and what kinds do not. They have ideas about what bits go in before others, and how they should be arranged after they get into the US box. These notions and ideas include things like: how much, when, how fast, where, and so on. It is rather like a recipe or master plan for relationships that we carry around in our head. It lets us know what we should expect from each other and how we should behave toward each other. The blueprint process is, typically, not something that people give a great deal of thought to. Everyone knows, we assume, what a marriage should be like. Similarly, women have notions about what men are like; for example, they drive the car, are responsible for the bills, are perhaps more logical than women, prefer showers to baths, mow the yard if there is one, have their favorite chair, like baseball games, enjoy drinking beer with their peers, and so on. Men have notions about what women are like; for example, they are supposed to clean the house, are more emotional than men, don't enjoy sex as much as husbands, like soap operas, gossip a lot, don't need as much rest, don't work as hard, really want their husbands to be the boss, and so on. Parents have blueprints about what kids are like. Children develop a blueprint for parents. Everyone develops a blueprint for friends. Boys have a blueprint for US boxes with girls, and girls have one for US boxes with boys. The list could be continued on and on. Everyone has a supply of blueprints for use in a very wide range of US box situations.

These ready-made blueprints present some problems, however. Some people have one specific blueprint that they try to make fit in every relationship situation. They try to relate to everyone in the same way. "I'm always the same. I just can't understand why many of my relationships don't work." This is somewhat like a man who learns one part in a play and spends his entire life playing that one role. The problem is, of course, that the play changes. He becomes involved in many different kinds of relationships, a variety of social situations, and numerous US boxes. The problem is compounded when two individuals try to use separate, ready-made blueprints for their relationship. If one individual has specific ideas, notions, beliefs, thoughts, and so on, about how the relationship should be and the other person has different notions, ideas, and so on, the US box will never grow. It is rather like two architects trying to build a skyscraper and a football stadium on the same land, at the same time, with the same materials. Individuals involved in trying to build an US box with different blueprints have a problem. One of them will probably insist that the other's blueprint is wrong; the other will assume that he has the only right way to do it. In other situations, the individuals may start out with one mutually acceptable blueprint. The problem is that they either do not stick with it or change blueprints without discussing it with each other.

These people might be thought of as blueprint switchers. "I've tried everything I can think of to get along with you, and nothing seems to work." When you hear someone say that, it is a good sign that he is a blueprint switcher; He first tried one way or plan, then another, then another, and so on. The problem is, of course, that he did not bother to tell anyone that he was switching blueprints. Also, if we think about the architects, it wouldn't work very well, either, if they were to compromise by agreeing to work for a few days building a skyscraper and then continue for the next few days to build a football stadium; the result would be neither a skyscraper nor a football stadium. It would, however, be a mess. A special note, "I've tried everything, and nothing seems to work" is frequently heard as parents talk about the ways they have tried to deal with their children. If the parents really have tried everything, it is sad to think about how truly confused the children must be. Other signs of blueprint switching are: "We either fight or don't speak to each other" or "I never know what mood he'll be in." Examples of blueprint switching are, of course, endless. Some people do it all of the time. Other people do it very seldom. If individuals are trying to build a satisfying US box, however, they must be very careful with the blueprint process. They will need to expand their US box building contract to include some final agreements.

10. We will agree about the blueprint process, including a clear understanding of the kind of US box we are building.
11. If we have different blueprints for the kind of US box we are building, we will not become involved in the building process until we have agreed to use one or the other of our blueprints or a new and mutually acceptable blueprint.
12. Once we have agreed on a blueprint process, we will both stick with it and will only switch blueprints after considerable discussion and after agreeing to the switch.

ACTIVITY 17

ORIENTATION OF SPOUSES TO EACH OTHER

THIS ACTIVITY is designed to facilitate your thinking about you and your spouse in terms of the orientation of each of you. It will be helpful to think about orientation as simply a reflection of individual style. On the dotted line between the ends of each scale below, put an X toward the end that best characterizes you. Put a Y toward the end that best characterizes your spouse. If you believe that either of you falls about the middle, put the X or Y toward the middle. Once you have followed this process for each of the nine scales, think about what the implications are for each of you and for your relationship with each other. What do you think the strong points are that result from your individual orientations? What do you think the problematic points are that result?

It will also be helpful if your spouse completes this activity. This will give each of you an opportunity to share your perceptions of yourselves and of each other. Remember that your orientation is simply a matter of style. It is neither positive nor negative, good nor bad. It simply represents a dynamic or factor within your relationship that influences how you perceive and relate to each other.

Once you have completed the activity to this point, go back and put a Z on the line where you feel you would like to be with respect to each scale. The difference between where you think you are and where you would like to be represents an important area where you will be able to invest personal time and energy in enhancing your personal style and your relationship with your spouse.

1. More dependent . . . . .More independent
2. More people oriented . . . . .More task oriented
3. More oriented to approaching people . . . . .More oriented to withdrawing from people

4. More oriented to affiliation and involvement with others .... More oriented to personal achievement and success
5. More oriented to the quality of experience and activities .... More oriented to the effectiveness of experiences and activities
6. More oriented to details and fine points .... More oriented to generalities and the bigger picture
7. More optimistic.................................. More pessimistic
8. More oriented to security .... More oriented to opportunity
9. More oriented to consistency and predictability .... More oriented to excitement and spontaneity

DISCUSSION

A lot of misunderstandings, misperceptions, and negative interpretations within marriage result from fundamental differences in the orientation of each partner to the other in terms of the variables introduced in the activity. Dependent/independent orientation is, perhaps, key here. Individuals with more of a dependent or follower orientation are sometimes seen by more independent individuals as emotionally draining, not accepting responsibility, and as not showing enough initiative or self-direction. Alternatively, individuals with a more independent orientation are sometimes seen as stubborn, self-centered, insensitive, and as inconsiderate of the feelings and interest of other people. The key is that these "labels" are simply negative interpretations of the styles of individuals.

Within the marriage relationship, these negative labels and interpretations become sources of conflict, tension, and negative pressure on the relationship. Significantly, the variable (dependent/independent) parallels the "Psychology of Sharks and Seals" activity introduced earlier. Using the RECIPES approach already introduced, the consultant will want to work with the client relative to the client's orientation, his interpretation of the orientation of his spouse, the effects of the orientation difference within their marriage, and the counterproductiveness of negative labeling and interpretations. In addition to following the suggestions in the "Sharks and Seals" activity, the consultant and the client may want to look for areas in which more dependent clients may function more independently and more independent clients may function more cooperatively and reflect more mutuality in terms of actions and decision making.

As the consultant works with clients relative to this element of marriage, one of the common themes is, "I am just an independent person."

Importantly, clients need to learn that this represents a position as opposed to a shared interest—with this differentiation being discussed in a later activity related to negotiating. At its essence, the position says, "I am an independent person—and as one might expect from an independent person—you may take it or leave it." Dependent individuals take what is a similarly nonnegotiable position, "I am a dependent person and have always been so. I just get overwhelmed and can't handle being more independent and not being able to count on you. It is just not my nature to want to control everyone and tell everyone what to do."

These same consultation issues arise with respect to individuals more oriented to people and those more oriented to tasks. Just as an appropriate marriage balance is needed with respect to dependent/independent orientation, a people/tasks balance is also important. With respect to independent/independent orientation, each spouse needs at times to be more dependent and at times more independent. Similarly, each needs to at times be more people-oriented and at times more task-oriented.

People-oriented individuals are very focused in terms of feelings, socioemotional comfort, consideration of the needs and interest of others, and place high value on the relationship and on the interpersonal gain within the relationship. The central theme is loving each other, caring about each other, and relating to each other. Task-oriented individuals focus on getting things done, following through with responsibilities, and the active/doing aspect of the relationship.

The negative labeling process already discussed becomes the first issue, with developing a middle ground being the goal. What usually is seen through consultation is that both individuals are oriented to people and both to task. The only real difference is the priority given to each side of the continuum. Marriage effective functioning comes, with the assistance of the consultant, through selective orientation sometimes more to the people aspects and sometimes more to the task aspects, with the effect over time being an orientation to both in an approximately equal measure.

The remaining seven orientation variables need to be understood and managed in much the same ways as have been suggested for dependence/independence and people/task. Some individuals are more approach oriented, more outgoing, more initiating with respect to physical, social, sexual, and intellectual interaction while others are more withdrawing oriented, more oriented to waiting on others to "bring the relationship to them." Who usually starts conversations? Who usually initiates social activities? Who usually is the more active participant sexually? Who is usually first to begin discussions around significant issues and topics? Through consultation, the individual may learn to strike a balance within the marriage, adopt an approach/withdraw pattern that is more comfortable for him and to which his spouse may more comfortably respond. Importantly, developing the skills and insights necessary to develop the balance being discussed here is in the interest of increased marriage effectiveness for the individual and also in terms of increased satisfaction with regard to the responses received from the spouse. Marriage is a two-way street. Developing more effective marriage behavior and skills more nearly assures that the individual will receive the benefits of action moving both ways on the marriage street.

Affiliation/achievement as an orientation variable may be understood somewhat in terms of a combination of people/task and approach/withdrawal as orientation variables. Those oriented to affiliation place high value on the relationship, interaction, and so on, while those more oriented to achievement place high value on accomplishment, "improving" the relationship, and so on. Importantly, an individual who is totally affiliation-oriented may minimize the importance of sexual skill and effective sexual involvement, while an individual emphasizing achievement might primarily focus on some held standard for sexual excellence. The point is that the consultant must take care to help the client understand the behavioral and situational correlates of his orientation.

An orientation variable that frequently causes problems within marriage deals with the relative orientation to detail or generalities. This is probably best observed when listening to an individual relate an experience, explain something or talk about a specific situation or event. The individual oriented to detail will go into a very exacting process, being sure that every element, every issue, every component event is included. For individuals having a more "generality" orientation, listening then becomes very tedious, time consuming, and difficult. They become impatient, frustrated, and show a real inclination to hurry the detail person along, finish comments and explanations for him, and generally speed things up. Conversely, the individual oriented toward generalities will be accused of not being open, not caring enough to really talk about what is happening, and not really being interested enough. The fact is that these are just simply different orientations to the thinking process, the analysis process, the understanding process, and the communication process.

The above discussion relative to developing balance is relevant here. In addition, both patience and tolerance become very important. The detail person needs to learn to give and ask for less detail, only the level of detail that really is necessary or essential. The person oriented to generality needs to learn to slow down, be a little more concrete, and to both give and request enough detail to be sure he really does understand and that his spouse is comfortable with the interacting communication process.

Given the above discussion, the client's orientation to optimism versus pessimism needs little elaboration here. There is one point that might be overlooked, however. Optimism becomes an energy source or positive driver that enables the couple to deal with problems, difficulties, and special situations that come up from time to time. It is the "better day" that helps one get through the difficult or ambiguous times. Alternatively, some degree of pessimism is healthy and useful. It encourages the couple to be somewhat more cautious, to plan more thoroughly, and to be a little more prepared for the difficult or problematic times. It is, however, an energy drainer in respect to the relationship. Pessimism should be at a level that serves its positive purpose without becoming a burden to the relationship and continuing interaction.

An orientation to security versus opportunity develops problematic interpersonal gain in many marriages. Security is, of course, an important element within the marriage and is one of the positive motivating factors for being married. Security needs to be assured, to the extent that that is possible, then. At the same time, though, life in general and marriage in particular has certain inherent risks, certain chances that one takes. To avoid all risks, to take no chances in fact reduces the probability of future security. If one deals with things too cautiously, the opportunity for improved security in the future is lessened. It can be seen, thus, that security and opportunity are interdependent and coexistent. Disproportional emphasis on either jeopardizes the other. The marriage effective couple manages the security/opportunity balance in ways that maximize both while minimizing jeopardy to either.

Finally, consistency versus excitement is an orientation variable that has a problematic potential within marriage equal to or greater than any of the other orientation variables. "Variety" might have as well been used as "excitement," since positive variety is generally the main ingredient in excitement. When couples indicate that their marriage is dull and boring, one way of thinking about that is that the relationship has become quite consistent and extremely predictable. In this sense, then, the alternative to "dull and boring" is positive variety with the added benefit of additional excitement. This is, of course, an operational element in the lover/sexual domain within the marriage but also should be understood as important within the "friends" domain. Variety here comes through variation in activities, conversational topics, other people with whom the couple interacts, and so on. It may be true that variety really is the spice of life. Importantly, though, a significant level of consistency and predictability is also essential. The key then is a balance of predictability and variety, consistency and excitement.

An orientation to quality versus effectiveness is considered here out of order emphasizing its importance to and relationship to each of the other eight orientations. Individuals oriented to quality within the friends', lovers', or partners' domains give priority to feelings, satisfaction, comfortableness, and interpersonal gain. At the same time, they tend to understand things in terms of some standard of perfection or excellence to which people, actions, and events are to conform. This is what they mean by "quality."

Those more oriented to effectiveness emphasize getting the job done, reaching the goal, or doing what works. It is, to some extent, the old dilemma, means versus ends. Those oriented to quality are more oriented to the means and to the extent to which the end conforms to some standard. Those oriented to effectiveness are less concerned about means and concerned about ends primarily in terms of whether or not they satisfy what was wanted, needed, or expected.

"When we do something, is highest priority placed on how we do it and how it turns out or on what we do and what the outcome is?" In all areas of marriage, including the other eight orientation variables, the key within effective relationships is developing a balance that values both the means and the end, values both quality and effectiveness. The consultant will want to work with the individual or couple in this area moving toward an orientation that emphasizes both quality and effectiveness in relationship to; people and tasks, detail and generality, the more active and the less active role, security and excitement, and so on. Marriage effective couples emphasize both quality and effectiveness within all three marriage domains: friends, lovers, and partners.

The consultant may wish to extend this activity by raising some additional questions.

1. Which two of your orientations are you most—least—comfortable with and find most essential to being who you are? Which two of the orientation elements of your spouse are you the most—least—comfortable with? How does this affect your relationship?
2. Discuss how you go about letting your spouse know about your orientations. How do your orientations show up through your behavior, actions, pattern of interacting, and so on?
3. How do you develop a balance of orientation, sometimes reflecting an orientation more toward the elements on the left side as listed in the activity and sometimes more toward the elements on the right side? How does this effort show up in your behavior, actions, ways of doing things, and so on?
4. How do you take your spouse's orientation into consideration as the two of you relate, work together, participate in your family, and so on?

ACTIVITY 18

MARRIAGE BALANCE

THIS ACTIVITY combines and extends some of the elements of earlier activities, especially those related to individual style. It is also similar to the last activity insofar as you are being encouraged to think about yourself, your spouse, and how the style of each of you contributes to your relationship. It is important to keep in mind that the balance elements discussed in this activity are not good or bad, right or wrong. Looking at each element in terms of you and your spouse simply helps to better understand your relationship and better manage your participation in the relationship.

Each of the elements below represents an interactive point within your marriage. Here, put an X beside of the element if you think that it reflects a stronger area for you than for your spouse, a Y if you think that it represents a stronger area for your spouse than for you, and a Z if you think the two of you are about equal with respect to the element. X equals stronger for you—Y equals stronger for your spouse—Z equals about the same for each of you.

Once you have finished, it may be helpful to make three lists. The first list includes all of the elements you have marked X. The second list includes all of those marked Y, with the third list including all of those marked Z. This begins to give you a picture of the participation of each of you in your marriage. It will also be good to share this activity with your spouse, if he/she wants to participate.

1. ___Being clear about what is expected.
2. ___Working well with the other.
3. ___Dealing with the ups and downs.
4. ___Showing pride in the other.
5. ___Being supportive.
6. ___Being open and upfront.
7. ___Listening.
8. ___Accepting the other.

9. ___Not blaming or accusing the other.
10. ___Keeping commitments.
11. ___Keeping criticism minimal and specific.
12. ___Being predictable.
13. ___Being helpful.
14. ___Valuing your relationship.
15. ___Having faith in the other.
16. ___Staying involved with the other.
17. ___Talking with the other.
18. ___Giving your marriage his/her best shot.
19. ___Being patient.
20. ___Dealing with the give and take of your relationship.
21. ___Depending on the other.
22. ___Not trying to boss or control the other.
23. ___Understanding what the other needs.
24. ___Being gentle.
25. ___Helping the other feel special.
26. ___Satisfying the other.
27. ___Accepting the other's bad days.
28. ___Having time for the other.
29. ___Encouraging the other's interest.
30. ___Not over reacting or getting upset too easily.
31. ___Being a good example or model for the other.
32. ___Being flexible.
33. ___Paying attention to the other.
34. ___Adjusting to the other.
35. ___Conveying interest in the other.
36. ___Being tolerant of the other's habits and moods.
37. ___Resolving and working out problems.
38. ___Being positive and constructive.

DISCUSSION

Many of the elements in this activity have been raised and discussed in Part Two of this book. They are here being specifically applied to the marriage relationship, keeping in mind that marriage includes being friends, being partners, and being lovers. Each element in the activity should, then, be considered in terms of the individual's functioning within the core triangle—friends, partners, lovers.

Since many of the elements have been previously discussed and several are self-explanatory, this section will only focus on a few of the elements, highlighting points that might be overlooked and points warranting special consultation attention. The consultant will want to take care to incorporate those points raised in earlier discussion sections.

Being helpful to each other is a straight forward concept. Its application to being friends and being lovers is sometimes overlooked, however. Within the friendship dimension, the client needs to be sure that she is doing all she can do to facilitate activities, social opportunities, comfortable communication, and a sincere friendship orientation. Within the lovers dimension, being helpful includes doing what one can to increase the comfort and satisfaction levels of her spouse, modeling an appropriate level of sexual initiative and skill, and responding to the sexual needs and interest of the other. The idea is that being helpful implies facilitating the involvement and satisfaction of one's spouse.

Valuing the relationship is more complex than one might first think. Of course, this includes communicating one's valuing of the relationship to the marriage participant but also includes communicating valuing in ways that are understood and valued by the spouse. "What kinds of things do you interpret as indicating that your spouse values the relationship? What kinds of things does your spouse interpret as meaning that you value the relationship?" It is not enough to simply value the relationship. This valuing must be communicated in ways that are understood and meaningful from the other person's point of view. Priority might be given to being helpful but also might be seen in terms of hanging in there and dealing with the ups and downs or in terms of manifestations of acceptance and faith in the other person. The notion is that valuing of the relationship needs to be communicated. This communication, in turn, comes through some prioritized mix of the elements in this activity.

Talking with each other is a similarly complex component of the marriage interaction. How one talks, how often one talks, what one talks about, and how responsive the talking is to the other person are all important ingredients. It is not enough to simply talk. One must "communicate" with the talking focusing on each dimension of the core triad and on what is really going on at a day-to-day level. In addition, talking needs to expand to dreams, fears, hopes, asperations, frustrations, and the full range of life and living.

Talking is for the purpose of conveying what is happening with the individual but also has the equally important purpose of letting the other person know that she is acknowledged, understood, and appreciated. The consultant will want to work with the individual in terms of assuring that talking is considerably more than just talk.

Accepting the other person as she is or as he is may be one of the toughest parts of marriage effective functioning. When all is said and done, people are not going to change very much. Either they are accepted "pretty much" as they are or they are to spend their lives being, to some extent, rejected. Keep in mind that, if one is not accepted, the experience for the individual is one of being rejected. People can become more effective friends, more effective partners, and more effective lovers. Nonetheless, who they fundamentally are is not going to change very much. Expecting the other person to become more skilled and more effective is reasonable. To not accept her on a relatively as-is basis, though, is an exercise in frustration for both spouses and is probably one of the quickest ways to sabotage and undermine the ongoing growth of the marriage.

The above, at its essence, brings into central focus the importance of each spouse being able to depend on the other. Yes, this includes depending on the other to do things, keep commitments, and be there when needed. More fundamentally, though, depending on the other person also includes knowing that she really does understand your needs and interest, will not turn on you, accepts you on an as-is basis, will help you feel special and important, and is a worthy guardian of your self-esteem and self-respect.

Adjusting to each other within a marriage relationship is a central factor in the success of that relationship. Many times, couples will understand this as "compromising." The reality is that people do not actually compromise very often and then usually only with some sense of frustration and a sense of having given up or given away something important. Adjusting to each other is not the same as compromising, then. It is, rather, a process of understanding each other's priorities, preferences, and idiosyncrasies. Each spouse then adjusts and accommodates to the style of the other in ways that encourage and facilitate the styles of each, without requiring either to give up things or elements of self that are important and valued.

The real skill here is coming up with arrangements and approaches that do not require either spouse to compromise or give up things that are important. The creative arrangement is such that both are able to be who they are, with style, all the time, on purpose. The only expectation is that both individuals are people with style and that the style of each reflects a positive sense of self and orientation to the other. Important here is the idea of interest which will be discussed in more detail in the activity dealing with negotiating.

Being positive and constructive in the context of representing a good interpersonal model may be thought of as incorporating and summarizing each of the balance elements in the activity. The consultant may help the client use the RECIPES approach to her marriage functioning especially in terms of recognizing positive participation in the marriage as contrasted with negative, destructive, or counterproductive participation. It is fair to first judge any incident or event in terms of the client's functioning and to judge that functioning based on its positive, constructive contribution to the relationship and on the extent to which it may serve as a model or guide for future functioning.

ACTIVITY 19

MARRIAGE ASSESSMENT

THIS ACTIVITY is designed to help you assess your marriage relationship. For each of the statements below, rate yourself using a scale from five to one. Five equals almost always, four equals usually, three equals sometimes, two equals seldom, and one equals almost never. Once you have finished rating yourself in terms of all of the items, add your ratings together and divide the total by fifteen. The result will be a marriage score. Generally, marriage scores of 4.0 or higher are found in happy, successful marriages. Importantly, though, you will want to give attention to any item where you have given yourself a rating of three or less and especially to those items where you have given yourself a rating of two or less. In these cases, the first step is to talk about the marriage area with your partner. The next step is to talk with your marriage consultant about the specific problem area. He/she will have advice and suggestions specifically related to this marital area. Following the suggestions will lead to your being more effective with that specific area.

Anytime you are experiencing difficulties within your marriage, keep in mind that the only thing you can do is to be the most skilled, the most effective friend-partner-lover you are capable of being. Go back to this activity, rate yourself and be sure to maintain your personal marriage score at a 4.0 level or above for two or three months, being very careful that no area continues at a level under 3.0. Also be sure that you are giving equal attention and emphasis to all three core dimensions: to being a friend, to being a partner, and to being a lover. Neglecting one of these core dimensions or putting off working on it is equivalent to deciding to let your marriage fail.

___ 1. I am clear about what is most important to me in my marriage.
___ 2. I have good personal habits.
___ 3. I am fun to be around.

___ 4. I am willing to take the first step to improve things in my marriage.
___ 5. I keep hassles and arguments short, to the point and under control.
___ 6. I do not try to change my partner.
___ 7. I am open and up front with my partner about what I think and feel.
___ 8. I am clear about what my partner sees as most important in our marriage.
___ 9. I manage involvements and relationships with relatives (or ex-relatives) in ways that make sure they do not interfere with my marriage.
___10. I am a good money manager.
___11. I do my share to keep our bills from getting out of control.
___12. I am sexually skilled.
___13. I enjoy sex with my partner.
___14. My partner enjoys sex with me.
___15. If I were my partner, I would like being married to me.

DISCUSSION

This activity should be considered in conjunction with the next three activities. Collectively, they are at the heart of effective marriage participation. This activity samples the elements from the next three activities, viewing the sample as representative of the individual's marriage effective functioning. If both the individual and his spouse rate the client high on all fifteen elements in this activity, she is clearly a marriage effective individual. If not, attention to the next three activities will serve to clarify and expand on any problems or issues raised through consideration of this activity.

The next three activities—being friends, being partners, and being lovers—stand alone without discussion sections. The experience and expertise of the consultant need to be a rich source of information, suggestions, and specific advise. In addition, the bibliography at the end of the book is a rich source of additional materials. At the same time, though, the consultant must be prepared to enlist the services of supplementary consultants who specialize in the specific interpersonal areas needing additional attention. Simply keep in mind that the approach is educational, competence-based, and oriented to increasing skill and interpersonal effectiveness.

Focusing on the current activity, the individual's being clear about what is important to him within the marriage should always be one of the first focal areas within the process involving the individual and the consultant. In fact, this area should be discussed even if the individual and his spouse see no particular problem here.

The client should articulate the four or five things that are most important to him, the most important benefits of being married. Similarly, clarity should be developed in terms of what is most important to his spouse.

Suppose that each spouse has five items on their "most important" list. It may be that some items appear on both lists, although the consultant will find that almost always there are items on each list that are not on the other. The result is ordinarily a list of seven or eight factors that the couple have on their "most important" list when the two lists are combined. Here is the critical factor. For the marriage to be successful, all of the elements on the combined list need to be understood and responded to in the marriage if the marriage is to be successful. Both individuals need to derive from the marriage all that they see as really important. At an importantly fundamental level, this is what they understand as a successful marriage: deriving those benefits that are viewed as most important. As a consultation focus, the consultant will want to incorporate all of these elements into the marriage enhancement plan.

Being fun to be around may be one of the most important qualitative ingredients within an effective marriage. In the last activity, attention was given to an orientation to quality versus effectiveness. Being fun to be around, of course, gives emphasis to the quality side of the variable, the quality of life within the marriage. A point for consultation focus relates to being fun in terms of its being a continuing and ever present factor in the marriage. Of course, there are those difficult times, times when things are frustrating, times when things are more serious. The perspective needs to be one that understands and takes into consideration the continuing nature of both the serious times and the fun times. They are interactive and continuous processes that represent important threads within "the tie that binds." Sometimes one is more apparent than the other. Over time, though, the importance of both fun and seriousness need equal attention. In fact, if one is going to be emphasized more than the other, the marriage would be well served if the balance is in favor of having fun and being fun to be around.

The last item in the activity incorporates and summarizes what may be the central and essential ingredient in being married with style, all the time, on purpose. "If I were my spouse, I would enjoy being married to me." Keep in mind the idea of style as being all the time, on purpose. "Would you always enjoy being married to you? Are you a model of effective marriage functioning? Would it be comfortable for you if your spouse were to function in a manner defined by your functioning for the next six months?"

Importantly, this does not mean that the spouse behaves exactly as the individual behaves. Rather, it means that the behavior of the spouse is based on the same assumptions, skills, attitudes, and priorities as are the behavior and functioning of the client. Almost always, a commitment on the part of the individual to marriage participation that meets this criterion has the effect of improved martial interaction and substantially increased socioemotional gain for both participants in the marriage.

Once this activity has been completed, the next three activities may be understood as behavioral mandates and as marriage effective criteria on which the client and the consultant may focus and through which they may move toward more effective and satisfying marriage involvement for the client. In short, the next three activities may be understood as a guide to relationship building within the core triad that constitutes the marriage, within the internal triangle.

ACTIVITY 20

FRIENDS WITHIN MARRIAGE

THIS ACTIVITY includes thirty statements related to being friends within marriage. As a dimension of the core triad, friendship is an essential element; and difficulties within the friendship relationship may have as much to do with the success or failure of the marriage as anything that may negatively impact the relationship.

Using a scale from five to one with five equals almost always, four equals usually, three equals sometimes, two equals seldom, and one equals almost never, rate yourself in terms of the thirty statements below. Each of the statements gets at an element in your friendship relationship with your spouse. Once you have finished, add your ratings together and divide by thirty. The result will be a friendship rating from 1.0 to 5.0. Marriage positive people usually maintain their friendship rating at 4.0 or higher. At any point you are experiencing difficulties in your marriage, go back to the thirty statements and spend a month or so assuring that your friendship rating remains above 4.0. Very frequently, this by itself will have very positive and beneficial effects within the marriage relationship. It will also be interesting to share your ratings with your spouse, comparing your perceptions of your friendship functioning with those of your spouse. Importantly, though, the goal of this activity is not for you to rate your spouse but to simply compare your self-rating with your spouse's rating of you.

___ 1. I am decisive and able to make up my mind about things.

___ 2. I am able to set priorities and decide what is and is not important.

___ 3. I am consistent and predictable.

___ 4. I am able to snap back from losses, disappointments, and those times when things do not work out the way I want them to work out.

___ 5. I have good personal habits.
___ 6. I am assertive with my spouse about what I want and need.
___ 7. I am fun to be around.
___ 8. I am gentle and tender with my spouse.
___ 9. I am relaxed.
___10. I am considerate of my spouse's feelings.
___11. I listen patiently and carefully.
___12. I am accepting and understanding with my spouse.
___13. I am willing to give my spouse the benefit of the doubt.
___14. I am willing to take the first step to improve things or to make things better.
___15. My spouse can count on me.
___16. I avoid blaming, threatening, or accusing my spouse.
___17. I am helpful to my spouse.
___18. I am clear with my spouse about what I want or need.
___19. I am positive and supportive with my spouse.
___20. I keep arguments and hassles short, to the point, and under control.
___21. I hang in there when there is conflict or tension in our relationship.
___22. I am tolerant of my spouse.
___23. I talk with my spouse.
___24. I spend time playing with my spouse.
___25. I am open and up front with my spouse.
___26. I deal with the ups and downs in our relationship.
___27. I have faith in my spouse and convey that faith to him/her.
___28. I am comfortable with and accept the changes in our relationship over time.
___29. I do not try to change my spouse.
___30. I am good at being a friend within our marriage.

ACTIVITY 21

PARTNERS IN MARRIAGE

THIS ACTIVITY works in the same way as the last activity, except this activity focuses on being partners within marriage. Use a five-point scale to rate yourself on each of the items in the activity with five equals almost always, four equals usually, three equals sometimes, two equals seldom, and one equals almost never. You will also notice that the items have been divided into subareas of the partner relationship. Please note that "being parents" is part of the partnership but is not discussed here, since that aspect of the partnership has been covered in detail earlier.

Once you have finished, add together your ratings for all partnership items and divide by the total number of statements. This will give you a partnership rating. The same technique can be used for developing a rating within each subsection of the partnership items below. The goal is to maintain a score of 4.0 or higher for all partnership items and within each partnership area. When problems develop, coming back to this activity will be a useful way of keying in on the problem points. Try to get your partnership rating up to 4.0 or higher and keep it there for two or three months as a way of positively responding to the problem points.

FINANCIAL

___ 1. I keep my bills under control.
___ 2. I effectively manage my money.
___ 3. I avoid unnecessary financial difficulties or obligations.
___ 4. I have and follow a budget.
___ 5. I am satisfied with the material possessions I have.
___ 6. I involve my spouse in major financial decisions.
___ 7. I understand and take care of my financial rights and responsibilities.

___ 8. I deal effectively with the financial difficulties that arise from time to time.

___ 9. I contribute my fair share to the financial dimension of our relationship.

___10. I am careful not to place too much or too little emphasis on financial matters.

BLENDING

___11. I understand and am sensitive to what my spouse wants for himself/herself.

___12. I am clear about what I want for myself outside of my marriage.

___13. I understand and respond to the special ways my spouse wants me to show love and caring.

___14. I understand how to be and am an active and involved participant in our marriage.

___15. I maintain healthy relationships and involvements with friends and relatives—including ex-relatives as appropriate.

___16. I relate comfortably and effectively to my stepchildren. (If not applicable, give yourself a rating of "4".)

ACTIVITY 22

LOVERS WITHIN MARRIAGE

THIS ACTIVITY is similar to the last two activities except the current activity focuses on you as a lover within your marriage. Using a scale from five to one with five equals almost always, four equals usually, three equals sometimes, two equals seldom, and one equals almost never, rate yourself on the statements below. Once you have finished, add your ratings together and divide by the total number of statements. The result will be a lover score from 1.0 to 5.0. Effective lovers within the marriage relationship maintain a lover's score of 4.0 or higher. If difficulties should develop in your marriage relationship, it will be useful to come back to this activity, rate yourself on the statements, and try to maintain a lover's score above 4.0 for a few months. Frequently, this part itself will result in significant improvement in the overall marriage relationship, including improvement in the friendship and partnership dimensions of the marriage.

___ 1. I am sexually attractive.
___ 2. I make sure that there are enough sexual opportunities.
___ 3. I anticipate sex with my spouse with pleasure.
___ 4. I talk with my spouse about my sexual wants and needs.
___ 5. I am careful not to place too much or too little emphasis on sex.
___ 6. I respond to my spouse's sexual wants and needs.
___ 7. Sex with my spouse is easy and comfortable.
___ 8. I am easily sexually aroused.
___ 9. I am sexually skilled.
___10. I function well sexually.
___11. I have good sexual timing.
___12. I accept my spouse's sexual values and beliefs.
___13. I do not make sexual demands on my spouse.

___14. I place more value on good feelings and a positive relationship than on specific sexual activities or techniques.

___15. I pursue sex with my partner only at appropriate times and in appropriate places.

___16. I remain sexually faithful to my spouse.

___17. I have let go of past sexual and/or romantic involvements and relationships.

___18. I do not accuse my spouse of inappropriate sexual or romantic activities or interest.

___19. I do not bring up past sexual or romantic involvements or relationships of mine or my spouse's.

ACTIVITY 23

TEACHING PEOPLE TO NEGOTIATE

BEING A GOOD negotiator is a skill you will find useful in many situations and especially as you participate in your family. The skills you will develop will facilitate your being more effectively assertive, being a better problem solver, and being a better conflict manager. Developing the skills is sometimes tedious and requires a lot of practice. The payoff is both substantial and positive, though.

At first, it will be useful to move through the negotiating process in a step by step manner. With practice and experience, you will gradually get to a point where effective negotiating is second nature to you and is not something that requires a lot of detailed activity. At first, though, it is important to develop a negotiating plan, to seek out opportunities to practice, and to work with your consultant as your coach and negotiating guide. It is a little like learning to play the piano. Learning how is tedious and time consuming. Being able to play well, however, is a very satisfying thing indeed.

PRELIMINARY ACTIVITIES

1. What do you want that I have, control, or can do? As odd as it may seem, this is frequently the step that inexperienced negotiators leave out. Very specifically, what do you want that I have? Here, we are talking about things, about concrete and tangible objects. What do you want that I control? Here we are talking about opportunities, resources, time, or other less tangible "things." What do you want me to do that I can do? Here, it is important to think in terms of things that anyone with my skills, in my position, and with my resources "can do." In very specific terms, what do you want from me?
2. With "it" referring to what you want, can I actually give it to you? This is another point that amateur negotiators frequently overlook.

What they want is something that the other person cannot, as a matter of individual choice, give to them. Perhaps other people are involved, maybe it is not something that the individual has the right or authority to simply give away, perhaps it is not something that the person can actually do, or maybe there are other factors that have to be taken into consideration other than simply deciding to give it to you. Under these conditions, simply negotiating with you is not enough, since I cannot simply give you what you want. Be sure that your negotiations are directed to the individual or people who can give it to you. Who all do you need to include in the negotiations? You should not leave anyone out.

3. Assuming I can give you what you want, under what conditions do you think I will give it to you? If you believe that I will simply give it to you without any conditions, there is nothing about which to negotiate. Simply ask me and I will give it to you. Here, though, let's assume that you think I will give it to you under some conditions. In specific terms, what are those conditions?
4. Under what conditions will you accept it—accept what you want—assuming I am willing to give it to you? Yes, you undoubtedly have conditions. Suppose you want to use my car for a week while yours is in the shop. It is my car, and I can let you use it. You think I will let you use it if you agree to take good care of it, bring it back with a full tank of gas, and you pay my bus fare for the week. Suppose my conditions are a little different, however. I agree to let you use my car for one week if you agree to make my car payments for one year. You will undoubtedly say, "No way." The point is that you do have conditions. Under what conditions will you accept what you want if I give it to you?

NEGOTIATING FOCUS

5. A successful negotiation is a conditional transaction. We do business under certain conditions. If you are still in the game to this point, you have a clear statement of what you want, a set of conditions that you think I will have in doing business, and your conditions for doing business. Make a chart with two columns with the left column including a list of your conditions and the right column including a list of my conditions. Now, what are the points of convergence: conditions on your list and on mine? The more points of

convergence there are, the further along the negotiations are going in. Your goal, of course, will be to reach a point where there is complete convergence, a point where the conditions on your list are the same as the conditions on my list.

6. What are the points of divergence: conditions that are on your list but are not on mine and conditions that are on my list but not on yours? Being careful to be very specific, now, make a master list that includes only our points of divergence, noting beside each point whether it is my condition or your condition. We will then negotiate our points of divergence.

As a central negotiating principle, keep in mind that you are never negotiating about what you want. That is a given and is actually nonnegotiable. If you did not want it, there is no point in pursuing it. We are simply negotiating the terms and conditions under which I will give it to you: our points of divergence. Amateur negotiators frequently fall into the trap of focusing on what they want. Skilled negotiators focus on the points of divergence: what we will call the transfer conditions.

CONSIDERATION AND LIMITS

7. What do you have, what do you control, or what can you do that would be of value to me? Look at my transfer conditions. You may use them as a guide for determining what may be of value to me in this particular negotiating situation. Make a list that includes what you can give to me in this particular negotiating situation. Make notation of why you think it would be of value to me. What benefits will I derive? What you give to me combined with the benefits I will derive from it represent the consideration you are offering in the negotiation.

As a summary point, you have determined what you want, have determined the transfer conditions, and now have determined what your consideration can be to induce me to follow through with the transfer. The stage for negotiating is set.

8. What are your negotiating limits? Review your list of consideration elements. Can you actually transfer control of them to me? What are the long and short term implications for you of making this transfer? Once you have considered the implications, revise your consideration list to include only those things you can give to me without jeopardizing yourself over time. This final list is what constitutes your negotiating limits: the maximum consideration you

are prepared to introduce into the negotiations. At no point, and especially not during a specific negotiating session, should you go beyond your negotiating limits, no matter how tempting it may be. Yes, you may miss an opportunity once in a great while. The advantage to you is this: making an unexpected offer you cannot refuse is a game run by truly skilled negotiators. Assume that he/she is at least as skilled as you are and is not about to "give away the store." What seems like an unexpected prize will usually turn out to be something for which you will pay dearly and without the benefit of prior thought or analysis. As good negotiators say, "Never come to the bait!"

9. Importantly, following all of the above steps gets you to what you think will be the final outcome of the negotiations. You think you will get what you want, the full consideration I have to offer. You have also determined your negotiating limits: the maximum consideration you will offer. If you want, simply make your best offer on a take it or leave it basis. This is, of course, not negotiating. It is rather simply making a nonnegotiable offer. What should you do if you want to negotiate, though? Simply list the preliminary transfer conditions: the least you are willing to accept and what you believe—hope—might be the least I would accept in return. These then represent the minimum transfer conditions. Negotiations now begin.

BEGINNING NEGOTIATING

10. Always start with a consideration for consideration offer: a presentation of the minimum transfer conditions well within your negotiating limits. Declare yourself up front. "You have something I want and I have something you want. I am a negotiator. Let's negotiate about the transfer conditions." For example, "I would like for you to . . . . I understand that it would be something that would change things a little for you. I think that I have an offer that will make it a comfortable thing for you, though. In consideration of your . . . , I will. . . ." Simply fill in your consideration and my consideration: the minimum transfer conditions. You have made me a consideration for consideration offer and have done so in a way that lets me know that you are a serious negotiator.

If I begin negotiating, all is well. I might say, "I might think about what you want from me; but what you're offering is not enough for me to give you what you want, you will need to . . . ." I have made a counter offer and we are "horse trading" as the negotiators say. Suppose I say, "No." Are the negotiations over? Being a good negotiator you understand my saying "No" as simply my first negotiation offer. You say, "That really surprises me. Under what conditions would you. . . ?" I will then probably make an opening offer—present an initial set of transfer conditions to you. If not, you simply learned that what you want is—from my point of view—simply not negotiable.

11. The following tips have been found by good negotiators to increase their negotiating effectiveness and increase the extent to which they are respected as effective negotiators.
    (a) Stay relaxed and friendly.
    (b) Remember the 80-20 rule. Eighty percent of the movement—progress—will be made in the last 20 percent of the time available for negotiating. Knowing this makes it easier to stay relaxed and much easier to be patient.
    (c) Keep your focus on the negotiations—the transfer conditions. Skilled negotiators will try to distract you, will talk about things unrelated to the negotiations, and try to diffuse your focus. Through this process, keep your internal focus, your mind's eye on the negotiations.
    (d) Ask for and suggest options. When suggesting options, raise—only as possibilities—different mixes or combinations of consideration. Here, it is important to take care to always stay within your negotiating limits.
    (e) Always remember that you are negotiating and never simply trying to get your own way. Your focus is on the transfer conditions and includes your giving me something in exchange for what you hope to get.
12. The following negotiating strategies appear subtle and not easily seen from the point of view of the negotiating novice. For a skilled negotiator like the one you are becoming, though, they are easy to spot and are an important part of your negotiating repertoire.
    (a) Use the first third of the available negotiating time simply to get a feel for my interest. Importantly, you will also determine what I want; but my interest represents how I think I will be better off if we are able to successfully complete our negotiations. "Interest" is not what I want but rather "Why" I want it.

(b) Once you have a feel for my interest, develop a priority listing of that interest as you understand it. Put my most important interest—my most important "Why"—at the top of the list and then continue listing my interest in terms of decending priority for me.

(c) Acknowledge and facilitate my interest in the priority order you have developed.

(d) Based on your understanding of my interest, take time to show me how I am going to be better off.

(e) As you talk about the transfer conditions, be very clear. Show me who, what, when, where, why, and—most importantly—how.

(f) Within any exchange—meeting transfer conditions—there are some risks. If there were no risks to me including no possibility of being less well off after I give you what you want, I would probably simply give it to you. I would understand that as doing you a favor and, if nothing else, would expect that you might reciprocate at some point in the future. When negotiating, there are always some risks. Be up front with me and very specific about the risks. Show me all of the risks. This will require that you think about the situation from my point of view, from my perspective. Good negotiators are superbly skilled with this aspect of the process. From my point of view, what are the risks? It is always better if you bring them up and define them clearly for me than if I bring them up in the process.

(g) As you interact with me, limit the amount of detail you bring into the process, be very accurate, and always have more detail available to expand on or back up anything you say. Wait for me to request the additional detail, though. If I do not request it, it is appropriate for you to indicate that more detail is available if I would like to have it. Let it go at this, though. (From a strategic point of view, this puts you in the position of being the expert who is teaching me.)

(h) Show me how we will share the risks and responsibilities. Remember that the person with whom you are negotiating will be more comfortable if the risks and responsibilities are shared as opposed to either your accepting all of the risk or responsibility or the other person accepting all of the risk or responsibility. From this perspective, the key is to maintain each of us as equal participants in the process.

(i) Always let me be the one to make the final decision. Even if I may have made the last offer and you are prepared to accept it say, "I think you have made an offer I can accept. I think we are about to a point where we can agree to agree. What do you think?" Whenever possible, let me make the final decision. Why? Because I will feel better, feel more in control, and feel more comfortable with the position into which you have gotten me.

(j) Always credit me with having made a good decision. Say, "I feel like you have made a really good decision. I appreciate the time you have spent talking with me about this." What if my decision was to simply stop negotiating and not do what you wanted me to do? The response is the same. "I appreciate the time you have taken to talk with me about this. All things considered, I think you have made a good decision from your point of view. It did not turn out quite the way I wanted it to turn out; but I respect the decision you have made." Why do this? You never know; you may want to negotiate with me again. You have left our relationship at a point where I will feel good about you and about negotiating with you again. Save your negative feelings or reactions for a later time when you are by yourself and can say anything you want to say. At the point our negotiations stop, though, take care not to "burn your bridges behind you," as they say.

ADVANCED NEGOTIATING TIPS

13. The following tips are used by serious and expert negotiators. Watch for them when negotiating. When they appear, know immediately that you are negotiating with an expert. Over time, you will find them becoming more and more a part of your negotiating style.

    (a) Be who you are with style, all the time, on purpose.

    (b) When you have gotten most of what you wanted while remaining within your negotiating limits, stop negotiating. Remember the 80-20 rule? It also applies here. You will almost always get about 80 percent of what you want; and trying to get the other 20 percent usually jeopardizes the 80 percent you have already gotten. This point backs off a little from an earlier point that said that what you want is not negotiable. For the beginner, this "what I want is not negotiable" point applies. For the expert, though, getting 80 percent of what you want 80 percent of the time you negotiate means that, over time, you will consistently get almost two-thirds of everything you want, which is probably at least 80 percent more than you have to have. It may not be the pot of gold at the end of the rainbow, but it is more than adequate for the good life.

(c) Never argue. Remember, you are a negotiator and arguing only lets the other person know that you are not a first-class negotiator. Let me argue if I wish. You negotiate with style, all the time, on purpose and understand that arguing is not negotiating.

(d) If you can avoid it, never let the negotiations reduce to a single issue. Never let negotiations reduce to a single condition either on your list or mine. If necessary, reintroduce a condition that seems to have already been resolved. Why? If there is only one issue, then it quickly becomes a simple yes or no decision. In this case, there is no further room for negotiating; and a box has been created. One of us has to decide yes or no. It becomes a "take it or leave it" proposition. As discussed earlier, if things get to this point, we are no longer negotiating. Keep enough issues "on the table" to assure that there is always negotiating content or "grist for the mill," as they say.

(e) Remember that people do not want the same things. You know someone is running a game on you if he/she says, "After all, we all want the same thing." This is virtually never true. You want to actualize your interest and I want to actualize mine. We may have some shared or common interest; but we will also have some interest that are not shared. As a skilled negotiator, you will recognize and acknowledge both our shared interest and those interest we hold as individuals.

(f) Understand and mention my needs, problems, and interest. When you do this, though, do not state them as facts. Say instead, "If I understand, you have a problem (need—interest) that I understand in this way. . . ." Once you have mentioned the problem as you understand it, ask me, "Does it seem to you like I understand or do we need to talk about this some more so I better understand?" Always convey a sense to me that I, my problems, my needs, and my interest are important to you and are being taken seriously by you.

(g) Always keep your focus on task—on the negotiations. Never shift focus to me or to personalities. Even when you are talking with me about your perceptions of my problems, needs, and interest, do so in ways that are related to our negotiations—to the transfer conditions.

(h) Focus on task with flexibility. If my style is to let the conversation drift, socialize, talk about other things, or to move away from task, "go with the flow." Always be personable, friendly, and interested. At the same time, though, look for opportunities to return to task gently, tactfully, and without becoming forceful or pushy.

SOME FINAL TIPS

14. Some final tips will help you polish your negotiating skills. The list below are seen frequently when negotiators are running a game. Watch for those times when the game is being run with you; and as your skill increases, you may want to carefully and cautiously run the game on the person with whom you are negotiating, although do this sparingly.

(a) Nibbling—you think that the negotiations are over. Just as we are about to commit to the agreement, I come back for a little more—a little nibble. The idea is to make you think that I might simply back out of the agreement if you do not go along with this little nibble, give me a little extra. Not responding to the nibble seems hardly worth jeopardizing the agreement. Just remember that a game is being run on you.

(b) Set aside—especially during the first 80 percent of the negotiating process, one or two issues tend to come up that seem insurmountable. This game suggests that you simply get me to agree to set that issue aside for a while, giving us time to work on other issues. The idea is that, once we have agreed on all the other issues, the one that was set aside will not seem that important or unmanageable. Also, we will have spent a lot of time and energy almost coming to agreement. The issue that was set aside then looms as a relatively small issue in relationship to everything that as already been accomplished. At that point, the self-perceived pressure is to agree on the issue that was set aside. It may, in fact, be the most important issue in the whole negotiation. Nonetheless, it usually gets resolved very quickly toward the end of the negotiating process. If the issue that is being set aside is really important to you, refuse to set it aside saying, "I think we need to deal with this now. We could agree about everything else; but if this is still in the way, we still have a problem. Let's talk about this now."

(c) Good guy/Bad guy—this comes up when you are negotiating with more than one person, keeping in mind that you include everyone in the negotiations who has any control or influence over the consideration sought. You are talking with one of the people and he/she says, "I would like to do this, would like to go along with you. The real problem is (put in the name of the other person involved). He/she is really hard to deal with about this. If you will go along with me on a couple of points, I will see if I can get him/her to go along with what you want." It is the old cartoon situation of the harried mother trying to get the youngster to cooperate. She says, "Either you deal with me now—cooperate with me—or you can 'wait till your father gets home.' "

(d) Reject the first offer—this is exactly what it sounds like, although sometimes it is not understood as simply a game someone is running. The person simply assumes that you have not made your best offer and rejects your first offer to induce you to improve on it. Instead of automatically improving on your first offer, then, you might say, "Wow! that really surprises me. That is about as good as I can do. Just out of curiosity, what kind of offer would you consider?" The other person then makes an offer. Running the same game, you say, "I'm sorry, I don't think I heard you correctly. You did not suggest. . . , did you?" The other person then indicates that this is what was said. You then say, "That is way beyond anything I can handle right now." He/she then says, "What could you handle?" You then say, "What I originally suggested is about all I can handle right now."

(e) Play dumb—at some point in the process we will get to a point where we are getting fairly close to agreement. If you were to give a little more or request a little less or if I were to give a little more or request a little less, we would be in agreement. Think about this in terms of money. Suppose you are at twelve dollars and I am at sixteen dollars. The temptation is to say, "Let's split the difference—let's compromise at fourteen dollars." Never do this. See if you can get me to do it. Say, "I can see that we are only four dollars apart. That's fairly close. I don't know what to do. Do you have any suggestions?" I will probably then suggest that we split the difference at fourteen dollars. You then say, "Well, that is surely better. I can see you're really trying to make this work. We are just about there. Being two dollars apart is not much. If we were just a little closer, I think I would be okay with the agreement. What do you suggest?" Just be sure not to push the game to far. Probably getting me someplace more toward you than simply splitting the difference is the point at which you should say, "You have definitely worked out something we can both be comfortable with. I think we should agree on the thirteen dollars you are suggesting. What do you think?" Never go for the "last ounce of flesh," as they say.

(f) The ice cream cone—you know you are dealing with an expert negotiator when this game is being run. I have an ice cream cone and you would like to have it. I am asking for a little more consideration than you are willing to offer. I say to you, "Why don't you go ahead and have a bite. If it is not just what you want, I'll keep what's left and you do not have to give me anything." My hope is that once you have tried it you will develop an immediate desire for the rest of the ice cream cone and will give me a little more than you had intended to offer so that you can have it now. Salesmen who offer a free home trial—with no obligation—are running this game. Youngsters who are skilled negotiators are also running the game when their offer is to do the dishes if you will reduce control over their activities enough to enable them to go to a movie. The youngster says, "I would like permission to go to the movie and thought that, since you are going to do this nice thing for me, I would do the dishes even though it is not my turn." The youngster has made a good consideration for consideration offer. You say, "No, I do not think that your going to the movie tonight is a good idea." The expert negotiator does not see this as a final decision. Rather, he/she runs the ice cream cone game. You go into the kitchen forty-five minutes later to find out the dishes have been done. If for some reason you did not go in, he/she will find some reason why you should come into the kitchen. You then see that the dishes are done and say, "Well, you went ahead and did the dishes. I told you that you could not go to the movie." Our junior negotiator then says, "I know, I just thought that doing the dishes would be a nice thing to do anyway." Will you simply say "thank you" or reconsider your "no movie" decision? As with other games, it was worth a try, from the young person's point of view.

(g) Willing to walk—never get into a position where you are not willing to walk, terminate the negotiations. If I ever get the impression that you will hang in there no matter what, you are totally at my mercy. At a minimum, I will probably be able to get you to give me more than you really wanted to give. Also, I will simply "dig in" and give no more than I have already offered. In fact, if I really believe that you will not walk, you may find me actually reducing my offer. Simply remember that, if you ever reach a point where you are unwilling to walk, the negotiations are over. The outcome is totally under my control.

(h) Horse trading—remember that 80 percent of the movement will occur during the final 20 percent of the process. Here we are talking about an old horse trading principle. Always save a little of your consideration for the final moments of the negotiating process. Do not run out of negotiating room until you get to the end of the negotiating process. Always have a couple of options left for horse trading. Another benefit is that I will leave the negotiation feeling that I got the last concession. That will make me feel a little smug and feel as if I am the superior negotiator. Among other things, this will probably lead to my underestimating you the next time we negotiate.

(i) Out waiting—the person with whom you are negotiating will gradually get a little frustrated and will want to move the process along. He/she will probably be impatient with only 20 percent of the progress being made during the first 80 percent of the available time. Here, the key is to relax, be patient, and simply out wait the other person. There is a strong likelihood that he/she will make an additional offer, increase his/her consideration, or do something else to move the process along. Just by being more patient and waiting, you have gotten more of what you wanted.

(j) Withdraw your offer—this is an easy game to run but must be managed very sparingly and very cautiously. Suppose you have offered to spend a half-hour with someone and he/she wants you to spend an hour. The negotiations seem to be reaching an impasse. You say, "Well, maybe it is just as well that we aren't coming to agreement about this. As I think about it, I'm not sure that I even have half-an-hour. Probably fifteen minutes or so is really all I can spare right now." The idea is that the other person will feel like the deal is getting away from him/her. Instead of holding out for the hour, he/she will grasp at the thirty minutes that seem to be slipping away. The other person says, "Wait a minute. You offered to spend a half-an-hour. I'm going to hold you to that." You say, "Well, I really do not have the time to spare; but since I did agree to a half-an-hour, I will be as good as my word. You have a half-an-hour."

(k) The reluctant dealer—this is a little bit like withdrawing the offer. Instead, you take the position that we can talk about this but that you are really reluctant to even consider it. "I have a lot of reservations about this. It is just something that I am not very comfortable with. We can talk about it; but I really don't think it is something I can handle at this point." The game is to get me to convince you not only why you should give up your consideration but why you should want and accept the consideration I am offering. This puts me in the position of needing to manage both sides of the negotiations, with your reluctant participation.

(l) The decoy—this game is run by true experts. It works like this. You make what you think is a simple, straightforward consideration for consideration offer. My goal is to complicate the negotiations. I do this by either making things seem like they are a lot more complicated than they really are or by introducing elements or issues into the negotiations that are not really relevant or at issue. I simply introduce them as if they were relevant or at issue, assuming that you will treat anything I say as relevant and important. For example, a teenager wants to use the car. He/she offers to buy the gas, be in by midnight, and wash the car before using it. A nice consideration for consideration offer. The parent, running the decoy game, says, "I don't know. You know that there was a really bad wreck last night and three youngsters were injured. I just don't know about your using the car." This is a pure decoy or what is sometimes referred to as a red herring. The problem for the youngster is to decide whether this is a negotiating game that is being run or if the parent is someone who just brings up irrelevant issues. The youngster says—being a good negotiator—"That was really a bad accident. You are like me. We are both still shocked about it. Is being in at twelve o'clock okay?" Good for our junior negotiator. Not only was the decoy parried, the comeback was one that simply assumed use of the car and moved the negotiations to the time to come home. With that kind of skill already shown, we can simply assume that twelve o'clock was well within the negotiating limit and that a somewhat earlier time would be acceptable." How did the negotiation end? As the youngster walked out the door to get into the car, the parent said, "Be careful and be sure to be in by eleven-thirty."

(m) A last trick in the game runner's bag—we have written what we hope has been a professional book that maintained the proper level of objectivity and style. Since we have come to the end, we thought that you might like to know about one additional game that may not quite maintain the professional demeanor that has been present to this point. This has been designated as "The Call Girl Principle." The principle says that the value of a service declines in direct proportion to the amount of time it has been since you have received the service. Of course, this is why the call girl always wants to be paid in advance. Good negotiators always make sure that there are definite arrangements made for how much they are going to receive and when they are going to receive it. Whenever possible, they receive it in advance. "You do what you are going to do for me and then I will do what I am going to do for you." By this point, though, you will undoubtedly be able to go the call girl principle one better. Try it when you and your spouse are in the lover's dimension of your marriage. What is this advanced principle called? You guessed it—simultaneous sex. As with many many things within family life, it is usually better to do it together than to take turns.

BIBLIOGRAPHY

Albert, Linda. *Coping With Kids and School: A Guide for Parents.* Ballantine Books, New York, N.Y., 1984.

Anderson, Carol M. and Susan Stewart. *Mastering Resistance: A Practical Guide to Family Therapy.* Guilford Press, New York, N.Y., 1983.

Andolfi, Maurizio, et al. *Behind the Family Mask: Therapeutic Change in Rigid Family Systems.* Brunner/Mazel, New York, N.Y., 1983.

Belkin, Gary S. and Norman Goodman. *Marriage, Family, and Intimate Relationships.* Rand McNally, Skokie, IL., 1980.

Blustein, Jeffrey. *Parents and Children: The Ethics of the Family.* Oxford University Press, New York, N.Y., 1982.

Brooks, Jane B. *The Process of Parenting.* Mayfield Publishing Co., Palo Alto, CA.

Cline, Victor B. *How to Make Your Child a Winner.* Walker & Co., New York, N.Y., 1980.

Coleman, James C. *Intimate Relationships, Marriage, and Family.* Bobbs-Merrill, Indianapolis, IN., 1984.

Cosby, Bill. *Fatherhood.* Introd. & Afterword by Alvin F. Poussaint. (A Dolphin Book). Doubleday, New York, N.Y., 1986.

Coulson, Robert. *Fighting Fair: Family Mediation Will Work for You.* Free Press, New York, N.Y., 1983.

Cox, Frank D. *Human Intimacy: Marriage, The Family and Its Meaning.* West St. Paul, MN., 1981.

Crow, Gary A. *Children at Risk.* Schocken Books, New York, N.Y., 1978.

Crow, Gary A. and Crow, Letha I. *Crisis Intervention and Suicide Prevention: Working With Children and Adolescents.* Charles C Thomas, Springfield, IL., 1987.

Curran, James P. and Peter M. Monti, Eds. *Social Skills Training: A Practical Handbook for Assessment and Treatment.* Guilford Press, New York, N.Y., 1982.

Draper, Thomas, et al. *See How They Grow: Concepts in Child Development and Parenting.* Butterick, New York, N.Y., 1980.

Edens, David. *Marriage, How to Have It the Way You Want It.* (A Spectrum Book). Prentice-Hall, Englewood Cliffs, N.Y., 1982.

Erickson, Gerald D. and Terrence P. Hmogan, Eds. *Family Therapy: An Introduction to Theory and Technique.* Brooks/Cole, Monterey, CA., 1981.

Faber, Adele and Elaine Mazlish. *How to Talk so Kids Will Listen & Listen so Kids Will Talk.* Avon Books, New York, N.Y., 1980.

Galvin, Kathleen M. and Bernard J. Brommel. *Family Communication: Cohesion and Change.* Scott, Foresman, Glenview, IL., 1982.

Garrett, William R. *Seasons of Marriage and Family Life.* Holt, Rinehart & Winston, New York, N.Y., 1982.

Gellert, Shepard D. *Nuts Come in Pairs: All You Wanted to Know About Couples, Relationships and Were Afraid to Ask!* Cite Press, Huntington Station, N.Y., 1983.

Goldenberg, Irene and Herbert Goldenberg. *Family Therapy: An Overview.* Brooks/Cole, Monterey, CA., 1980.

Gurman, Alan S. and David P. Kniskern, Eds. *Handbook of Family Therapy.* Brunner/Mazel, New York, N.Y., 1981.

Gurman, Alan S., Ed. *Questions & Answers in the Practice of Family Therapy. Volume 1.* Brunner/Mazel, New York, N.Y., 1981.

Gurman, Alan S., Ed. *Questions & Answers in the Practice of Family Therapy. Volume 2.* Brunner/Mazel, New York, N.Y., 1982.

Hoffman, Lynn. Foundations of Family Therapy: *A Conceptual Framework for Systems Change.* Basic Books, New York, N.Y., 1981.

Lamb, Michael E., Ed. *The Role of the Father in Child Development.* (Wiley Series on Personality Processes). John Wiley & Sons, New York, N.Y., 1981.

Lions Clubs International and the Quest National Center. *The Surprising Years: Understanding Your Changing Adolescent: A Book for Parents.* Quest National Center, Columbus, OH., 1985.

Maccoby, Eleanor E. *Social Development: Psychological Growth and the Parent-Child Relationship.* Harcourt Brace Jovanovich, San Diego, CA., 1980.

Mace, David R. *Close Companions: The Marriage Enrichment Handbook.* (1984) Continuum, New York, N.Y., 1982.

Madanes, Cloe. *Strategic Family Therapy.* Jossey-Bass, San Francisco, CA., 1982.

McGinnis, Alan Loy. *The Romance Factor.* Harper & Row, New York, N.Y., 1982.

McGoldrick, Monica, et al., Eds. *Ethnicity and Family Therapy.* (Guilford Family Therapy Series). Guilford Press, New York, N.Y., 1982.

Minuchin, Salvador and H. Charles Fishman. *Family Therapy Techniques.* Harvard Univ. Press, Cambridge, MA., 1981.

Mirkin, Marsha Prauder and Stuart L. Koman, Eds. *Handbook of Adolescents and Family Therapy.* Gardner Press, New York, N.Y., 1985.

Nichols, Michael P. *Family Therapy, Concepts and Methods.* Gardner Press, New York, N.Y., 1984.

O'Connor, Dagmar. *How to Make Love to the Same Person for the Rest of Your Life, and Still Love It.* Doubleday, New York, N.Y., 1985.

Okun, Barbara F. and Louis J. Rappaport. *Working With Families: An Introduction to Family Therapy.* Duxbury Press, Boston, MA., 1980.

Papp, Peggy. *The Process of Change.* (Family Therapy Series). Guilford Press, New York, N.Y., 1983.

Paul, James L., Ed. *Understanding and Working With Parents of Children With Special Needs.* Holt, Rinehart & Winston, New York, N.Y., 1981.

Powell, Douglas H. *Teenagers: When to Worry and What to Do.* Doubleday, New York, N.Y., 1986.

Rosenfeld, Jeffrey P. *Relationships: The Marriage and Family Reader.* Scott, Foresman, Glenview, IL., 1982.

Schulman, Michael and Eva Mekler. *Bringing Up a Moral Child: A New Approach for Teaching Your Child to be Kind, Just, and Responsible.* Addison-Wesley, Reading, MA., 1985.

Sears, William. *Creative Parenting: How to Use the New Continuum Concept to Raise Children Successfully From Birth Through Adolescenc* . . . Dodd, Mead, New York, N.Y., 1982.

Sedgwick, Rae. *Family Mental Health: Theory and Practice.* C.V. Mosby, St. Louis, MO., 1981.

Sell, Charles M. *Family Ministry: The Enrichment of Family Life Through the Church.* Zondervan, Grand Rapids, MI., 1981.

Singer, Laura J. and Barbara Lang Stern. *Stages: The Crises That Shape Your Marriage.* Grosset & Dunlap, New York, N.Y., 1980.

Stuart, Richard B. *Helping Couples Change: A Social Learning Approach to Marital Therapy.* (Guilford Family Therapy Series). Guilford Press, New York, N.Y., 1980.

Umbarger, Carter C. *Structural Family Therapy.* (Family Therapy). Grune & Stratton, Orlando, FL., 1983.

Weinhaus, Evonne and Karen Friedman. *Stop Struggling With Your Teen.* J.B. Speck Press, St. Louis, MO., 1984.

INDEX

N

O

P

R

S

T

DATE DUE

NOV 29 1989			
MAR 31 1994			
AUG 04 1994			
APR 16 1995			
NOV 29 1995			
JAN 2 1998			

DEMCO 38-297